To Charmaine

What's the Point of School?

How the current education system is failing to prepare students for the real world

JPAY

No part of this publication may be reproduced, stored or transmitted in any form or by any means, electronic, mechanical, photocopying, recording, scanning, or otherwise without written permission. It is illegal to copy this book, post it to a website, or distribute it by any other means without permission.

JP Ay asserts the moral right to be identified as the author of this work.

Copyright © 2020 JP Ay
All rights reserved

ISBN-13: 979 8 5665 2493 1
First Edition: November 2020

To my family and friends who always have faith in me and have supported me in writing this book

Thank you for purchasing this book!

It has been both fun and a challenge to create, and I have learned so much during the whole process. I am so glad that I was able to bring this project to completion, despite almost quitting twice, and can share this book with you.

Please do leave a review because I'd love to know your opinion and experience of school! Your help in spreading the word is greatly appreciated.

To contact me and for more resources, check out:
www.reformukschoolsnow.co.uk

CONTENTS

ABOUT THE AUTHOR 1
INTRODUCTION 7
FUNDAMENTALS 13
    MATHS 15
    ENGLISH 33
    SPORT 45
GCSES 53
    HUMANITIES 55
        GEOGRAPHY 56
        HISTORY 63
SCIENCE 75
    PHYSICS 77
    BIOLOGY 85
    CHEMISTRY 95

A-LEVEL	101
ECONOMICS	102
SO WHAT IS THE POINT OF SCHOOL?	123
MY REALISATIONS	135
APPENDIX – NUTRITION GUIDE	151
NOTES	155
REFERENCES	161
ACKNOWLEDGEMENTS	167

ABOUT THE AUTHOR

Who am I? More importantly, who am I to think I'm qualified to write this book?

That's a good question, with a simple answer. I'm a concerned student who's not only worried about my own future, but the future of the millions of students out there who believe that a good school education is the only tool they need when they leave the guided school system only to enter the real world with no destination.

My name is JP Ay, which is one of the shortest names in the world – although not the shortest, I checked. At the time of writing, during the summer of 2020, I'm transitioning between my 3rd and 4th Years of my MBiochem (Masters in Biochemistry) course at the University of Oxford. A course I've spent the past year debating whether or not to drop out of.

So why did I decide to write this book?

You might think I had a eureka moment; that a lightbulb flashed above my head and I realised that the school curriculum was partly to blame for drilling into every student's mind that they must become employees after leaving academia. However, in this situation, that isn't the case.

Rather, I had a series of realisations which eventually led me to question everything that I thought I knew. They convinced me that the current education system, which I once had complete faith in, has a lot to answer for.

I've written a detailed explanation of the experiences and realisations that brought me to these conclusions at the end of this book. But because this isn't about just me – it's about every student in the UK who's being failed by the current education system – we shall stay focused on the broader arguments first.

I was lucky enough to go to one of the best independent schools in the country, which provided me with a better quality of education than many, but I still felt unprepared for the real world when I left for university.

If I felt this way, coming from a school that took continuous pride in preparing the majority of their students for Oxbridge and Ivy League universities, I knew there must be other students going through the same difficulties, with far less advice, support and fewer resources than I was given.

Over the course of the past year, I've spent a lot of time debating whether to stay in or leave my degree, because I have become increasingly tired of rote-learning academic concepts for exams that have little to do with the real-world and spending no time learning real life-skills that are, I believe, essential to progressing in life.

I began to read a wide variety of books on the topics of financial education, psychology, body language, fake science and communication skills. With each book I realised how little these topics had been covered at school and they all had something to say about the wider world that I had never previously been exposed to. This led me to believe I was right about the failures of the current education model, which I believe is designed to prepare students for a narrow path through life. Collectively, they helped to show me why being the employee who slowly makes their way up the career hierarchy wasn't a long-term goal for me. And it confirmed my belief that the school system is often responsible for setting too many others on this path.

When I first mentioned to friends that I'd decided to write a book, many of them assumed that I was planning either a work of fiction or to explore some niche scientific topic (the latter is best left to academic dissertations, in my opinion); their reactions were non-committal.

However, when I explained that the book would be about my belief that the education system hadn't prepared us for the real world and the ways that the current curriculum should be reformed to better inform students like us about life beyond academia, that changed.

Every single one of them nodded their heads in agreement.

Granted, my friendship bubble might be quite Oxford-centric or academically orientated, so I didn't stop there. For a wider perspective, I set about to ask all sorts of people about school – from students at a cross-section of universities and others who didn't go at all, to current schoolteachers, employees, leading scientists and business leaders. I even spoke to someone who works for the Home Office.

All of them had interesting takes on the topic, and I am thankful for all their opinions and insights. In amongst their opinions, there was one main point that they all agreed upon: as it stands, the education system is in need of some sort of reform.

(The lack of critical thinking encouraged in schools was another common criticism: more on this later.)

So, now you join me at the present, sitting in a cafe with an iced mocha, laptop open in front of me, pondering how I got to where I am today.

I may still be a young, very much inexperienced student. I could have waited to 'walk-the-walk' before I 'talk-the-talk'. However, I believe I can share some of what I've observed and realised over the past few years NOW, at this moment. To pass on the mistakes that I've made and the lessons I've learned, in the hope others can learn from them too.

I am sure I'm not the first person to have come to these conclusions, nor do I hope to be the last. By reading this book, I hope that you, too, will have many 'Aha!' moments as you start to question all you thought you knew about much of what you learned at school and why I believe the curriculum is so flawed.

What's the Point of School?

INTRODUCTION

What's the point? Why? Do I have to do this? These are questions I'm sure you asked yourself or your parents on those mornings when you'd have to wake up, go to school for the whole day, then spend the evening sitting in front of a pile of homework, head in hands, tired and annoyed. And chances are you'd get a similar answer from your parents as the one I did: 'To set yourself up for later life.'

Working hard, knuckling down, powering through school – the theory goes that this paves the way to good grades, a job that pays well, and a happy life.

Well, I'd hate to smash this pretty life you're dreaming of, but it's a lie. It's time to question that dream, open your eyes and ask yourself: 'Does my school education really guarantee me a good future?'

I promise you, this book is going to help you see school from a very different perspective…

There are many reasons why following the familiar route of going to school in order to get a secure job until you retire doesn't actually work (pun intended). Every year, a huge wave of students leave education to enter the job market and yet only a few years after completing their A-Levels they could be earning tens of thousands of pounds apart from each other. Why?

You might think this is because of the decisions made by people once they have left formal education, and you would be partially right.

However, I believe that this misses a key point: school.

Yes, of course the quality of education across schools varies hugely, with state vs private educations being the most obvious point of difference. A private education can be an advantage; so is having private tuition and knowing and applying effective self-study techniques.

Nevertheless, I'm concerned with something much larger than the type of school you were in and the way you learn – something that applies no matter where you went to school.

What I'm going to highlight here are the inherent flaws of our educational system by way of the existing school curriculum. How it's failing to prepare students for the world beyond. How it's outdated and needs reform. How it guides you into the lie of following its course in the belief that by doing so you'll then be ready for the real world once you receive a piece of paper with an exam result.

Are you ready?

Let's look at the upsides first. (Yes, I know, surprisingly school does have a few!)

Schools provide many great opportunities to build relationship skills by being with other students and forging friendships and respect for others; they help show us how to work through challenging problems and, over time, develop the skills to be able to solve them with less and less guidance.

They provide a good structure to a work/play timetable, encouraging sport, some wider thinking, in subjects such as RS (Religious Studies) and PSHE (Personal, Social, Health and

Economic education), as well as extra-curricular activities and opportunities to take on leadership roles (e.g. prefects).

They give a sense of structure to academia and allow students to learn a lot of information in a short space of time, both in groups and independently. They provide structure to the lives of children and teenagers and provide them with activities to complete.

On the other hand, schools also encourage less beneficial behaviours which few students realise persist into their adult lives.

Some examples include:

- An absence of real teamwork to answer a problem.

- Working together to analyse ideas for a piece of individual homework is seen as cheating.

- Feelings of shame for doing badly on a test and/or making mistakes. Nobody can learn without making mistakes; they are a necessary part of progress.

- The need to cheat by looking up mark schemes and examiners reports for predicted upcoming mock exams.

- The common feeling that all information, regardless of whether you believe it to be right or wrong, is to be learned and regurgitated onto a test paper and immediately forgotten – imagine what would happen if taxi drivers, accountants or pilots followed this same principle.

From my experience as a student, I believe that an adherence to behaviours such as these – conscious or otherwise – can limit students' future successes as they progress through life.

So, what is success? The dictionary definition is 'achieving a desired outcome' or 'attaining wealth and/or fame'.

But this definition, as I'm sure you'll agree, is vague. We all have different ideas of what it means to be successful and to what extent fame, wealth, prestige, happiness, relationships and other personal goals play a part.

Does the desire for success arise from maintaining a moral and financial obligation to others or from a desire to be superior? Does it mean living a life of few regrets? It might be about being proud of accomplishing the goals you set. Or is it based on perceived self-worth? Perhaps you have a different definition in mind.

For the purpose of this book, I shall focus on financial success. I shall define this as being able to have the resources you need without having to work constantly, or in a job you hate, in order to support yourself and your future wellbeing. It means being in a position to be able to support others – both those who are close to you, such as family, friends, future partners and children, as well as those further away that you would like to help through donations to charitable causes.

The world that millennials and Generation Z are growing up in is very different to that of their parents. It's long been reported that millennials are likely to be the first generation unlikely to earn as much as their parents' generation[1]. They face rising unemployment coupled with ever-shorter job contracts with ever-fewer benefits and a housing market that for many remains firmly out of reach – and that was before the 2020 economic recession began to kick in.

And yet we're still being told to follow the same old rules and paths by our parents and at school: to pass exams and then work hard until retirement.

Not every student goes to university. Not all careers require a degree. As such I believe it's what we're taught at school and how we're taught it that is the most crucial to analyse if we want to redefine 'success' and the paths it could take to get there.

This book has been split into parts, following the current UK school curriculum Key Stages and goes through subjects from when they either first become compulsory or begin to be taught at a level where students are expected to complete assignments to consolidate their understanding.

I'm focusing on the UK school system as it's the one I have first-hand experience of.

However, with many educational systems around the world relatively similar in structure and approach, many of the arguments I'm presenting here are, I believe, broadly relevant and that my fundamental argument – that the modern education system is failing to do all it can to prepare *all* its students for the world beyond – resonates beyond the UK.

So, are you ready to revisit your school days and examine how you were failed by a curriculum designed to teach subjects purely to prepare for exams to obtain a piece of paper with your results rather than arm you with the skills you really need?

As you make your way through this book, you'll probably recognise and – I hope – understand many of the problems inherent within the current curriculum. But that's only the start of it.

The reason I wrote this book is to help you see a different approach to life. One that might even start you on a brand-new path. A path where you're no longer shackled by the constraints of the school system and its rigid process of learning for exam success over any other. Where you're free to discover a new set of tools that will genuinely and practically steer you towards a successful path of your own choosing through the big, bad, beautiful world.

I thought the best way for me to make my case would be to take you on a quick journey through your school life.

To provide you with further inspiration, I've added a short list of recommended reading to the end of some subjects – all of which serve as great supplementary material and offer information and perspectives not currently covered in school.

Let's start at the beginning with the very first concepts you would've learned at school – those aptly named fundamentals.

So, what are you waiting for?

Do you need someone to say, 'You may begin?'

FUNDAMENTALS

MATHS

1. $+ 1 = 2$

    This is the basis for all mathematics.

    It's simple, easy, and probably the very first equation you learned.

However, I bet you didn't know that it took mathematicians Alfred North Whitehead and Bertrand Russell 360 pages to conclusively prove it to be correct?[1]

Maths is a fundamental subject. It's one of the first ones we're taught and remains compulsory from the start of Primary School right up until the completion of Maths GCSEs.

A summary of the many topics you'll have learned over that period are listed below, ordered from KS1 requirements up to KS4 as listed on the GOV.UK website, updated on the 6th July 2020[2]:

KS1 (Years 1 – 2)
- Counting to 100
- Learning x2, x5 and x10 times tables
- Reading and writing numbers up to 20
- Basic Addition and Subtraction with two-digit numbers
- Basic Multiplication and Division

- Basic Fractions
- Measurements
- Telling the time
- Names of 2D and 3D shapes
- Solving problems using +, -, x and ÷
- Basic statistical charts

Lower KS2 (Years 3 – 4)
- Reading and writing numbers up to 1,000
- Adding and subtracting mentally, with three-digit numbers
- Knowing the 3, 4 and 8 times tables
- Additional fractions, measurements and geometry
- Learning about negative numbers and counting backwards
- Rounding numbers to nearest 10, 100 and 1,000
- Reading Roman numerals
- Using columns for addition and subtraction
- Knowing multiplication and division tables up to 12 x 12
- Converting fractions to decimals
- Converting between different units of measurements
- Classifying geometric shapes, and recognising symmetry

Upper KS2 (Years 5 – 6)
- Solve number problems with numbers up to a 1,000,000
- Add and subtract numbers with four digits
- Recognise and use prime numbers and squared/cubed numbers

WHAT'S THE POINT OF SCHOOL | 17

- Convert improper fractions to and from mixed numbers
- Utilise the % symbol
- Measure and calculate perimeter and area of basic 2D shapes
- Translate shapes on a graph and work out missing angles
- Read, write, order and compare numbers up to 10,000,000
- Use long multiplication and long division
- Identify common factors, common multiples and prime numbers
- Compare and order fractions
- Add, subtract and multiply simple pairs of proper fractions
- Use ratios and proportions to solve problems
- Express simple number problems algebraically
- Estimate areas and volumes of 2D and 3D shapes
- Build 2D from given dimensions and 3D shapes from nets
- Utilise pie charts and calculate the mean of data

KS3 (Years 7 - 9)

- Develop fluency, reason mathematically and solve numerical problems
- Use all four operations and understand their order (BIDMAS/BODMAS)
- Use real roots, inverse operations, and the standard form $A \times 10^n$
- Further algebra to solve linear equations in one variable
- Recognise arithmetic and geometric sequences
- Learn how to sleep through Maths lessons

- Further trigonometry, involving Pythagoras's theorem and angle facts
- Understand that probabilities sum to 1; use Venn diagrams
- Interpret and compare observed distributions of a single variable
- Describe simple mathematical variables between two variables

KS4 (Years 10 - 11)

- Consolidate numerical, algebraic and geometric reasoning and capabilities
- Explore limitations of mathematics and assess the validity of arguments
- Make connections between areas of mathematics to solve problems
- Calculate exactly with fractions, multiples of π (and surds)
- Factorise quadratic equations, and using functions with inputs and outputs
- Use $y = mx + c$ to identify lines and find parallel and perpendicular lines
- Solve quadratics and simultaneous equations; estimate answers with a graph
- Deduce nth term of sequences
- Understand inverse proportionality, set up and solve growth/decay problems
- Use terms such as chord, segment, radius, diameter, tangent, and arc
- Calculate surface areas and volumes of 3D shapes
- Know the exact values of sin, cos and tan for angles of 90, 180 and 360 degrees

- Describe translations as 2D vectors and add, subtract and multiply vectors
- Calculate the probability of independent and dependent combined events
- Interpret and construct tables, line graphs, and scatter graphs
- Recognise correlation and know that it does not indicate causation
- Interpret, analyse and compare the distributions of data sets from univariate empirical distributions

Well, that was a fun read, right? It doesn't even include the A-level Maths syllabus.

If you were handed this data on a form, you'd gloss over it as if it were the terms and conditions. (Often terms and conditions contain errors that you don't even notice; there's an irrelevant point in the list above, did you spot it?)

So, why did I list these numerical learning objectives?

Because they are all **compulsory** to learn.

And yet, how much of the above do you really remember? Or on a more frightening note, how much of the above have you used since?

Key Point #1: Not all maths is useful, but it has a lot more real-world applications that you might think

I'd like to make my own interpretation between useful mathematics and maths that you'd rarely, if ever, use again outside school.

In true mathematical fashion, I'll show this data in a table below:

USEFUL	IMMEDIATELY FORGETTEN
Mental arithmetic	Most geometry
Measurements (time, distance, etc…)	Irrational Numbers and Surds
Solving problems involving money	Trigonometry (sin, cos and tan may have some use in Physics)
Statistics	Sequences
Basic Algebra	Further Algebra
Data analysis and interpretation	Using formulae and mathematical symbols

The scale of 'usefulness' here has been selected by how often skills in those topic areas would be required beyond the school curriculum.

Some of these are obvious. Mental arithmetic, calculations involving money and using measurements are completed on almost an everyday basis; irrational numbers and surds, on the other hand, are unlikely to come up in a receipt or everyday calculation.

Even when you throw an object, which involves trigonometry, you rely upon your eye when aiming and throwing rather than taking out a protractor to perfect your aim.

Looking back, I'm sure you know which numerical skills you learned were useful and the ones that really, really weren't. The question is whether this scale of usefulness was ever raised in the current school curriculum.

I'd argue not. Topics such as statistics, for example, tend to be overlooked, even though they're very important in analysing and evaluating data, both academic and non-academic (more on this later).

It's my belief that students would benefit from more emphasis on practical areas of problem solving, critical thinking, analysis and data handling in the Maths curriculum – all of which, along with vital competencies such as communication skills, offer real-world application beyond school.

A pilot needs to be able to look at a map and calculate distances, and their spatial awareness is often tested with questions of selecting the correct 2D net pattern to make a 3D shape. A nurse or doctor needs to be able to calculate the correct dosage of a medicine to give to a patient, and how to change the volume if the concentration is altered. You use maths skills to plan a journey or event, make a purchase or know your personal measurements.

You don't need A-level Maths for any of these, but they do combine everyday mathematics with basic critical thinking skills – which is why this should be a fundamental part of any school mathematics course.

Many of the most useful life aspects of Mathematics will be learned 'on the job' when former students progress through life, but with such a vast array of real-world applications, why doesn't everyone have the opportunity to benefit from this learning at school?

Perhaps there could be a case study involving an analysis of potential investment choices for a hypothetical company, or even an introduction to savings, interest and how to look after personal finances (of which there's more on in the Economics chapter).

A solid foundation in mathematical reasoning will allow students to look beyond the exam questions and use Mathematics in life.

Key Point #2: Maths is a subject for everyone

People with degrees in Mathematics and Maths-related subjects often tend to work in finance, applying their skills to problems involving money, in roles such as accountancy, retail banking, investment banking and stock trading.

Real-world applications aside, a Maths A-level is a prerequisite for many university degree courses.

A Guardian Online report in August 2019 comparing numbers of students across a range of A-level courses revealed over 80,000 students completed Maths A-levels in both 2018 and 2019 – more than any other subject[3].

Impressive, right? However, if this data is then compared to an analysis by the FT in 2018, which indicated there were 20,000 more entries for A-level Maths from male students compared to female students, and that double the amount of male students completed Further Maths than female students (~11000 vs 5000), a different story begins to emerge[4].

There is an evident gender bias in those students taking up Maths beyond GCSEs.

Unfortunately, this gender inequality also applies to A-level subjects such as Physics and Engineering that, while slowly improving, suggests some entrenched social bias around female students studying STEM subjects at this level (and beyond) still remains.

Male or female, scientific research and engineering would not be possible without the use of maths. But many jobs require knowledge of Mathematics, it's not just a subject for geeks.

Or guys.

Key Point #3: Concepts should be learned for real-world applications rather than solely for marks in exams

Unless you intend to study Maths, Physics or Engineering at degree level, most Mathematics you learn at school will be forgotten the moment you complete the exam. Unlike other subjects, however, where this learning and forgetting has become expected, for Mathematics it can be detrimental as you move through life.

Let me give you an example. I recently visited a shop to purchase a few items using a promotional discount. The till system was offline and it took the shop assistant multiple attempts on her phone calculator to identify the correct price – a calculation that according to the curriculum summary previously outlined is expected of an 11-year-old.

Have we become too reliant on calculators to complete basic mental arithmetic involving numbers and percentages?

I'll bet I'm not the only person to have corrected a shop assistant because they've charged you the wrong price after trying to calculate the number in their head?

These are just a couple of examples of basic mathematical skills that have been quickly discarded by many adults upon leaving school – after all, as the reasoning goes: 'Why do something myself when this thing does it for me?'

And it's not just basic arithmetic that's quickly forgotten.

I've witnessed several arguments, both offline and online, over simple mathematical equations. Equations such as the one below:

$10 - 2 \times 6 \div 3$

If you think the answer is 16, well done, you've proven why these arguments start.

The correct answer here is 6.

The 'argument' comes down to a simple mathematical principle called BIDMAS (or you may have heard BODMAS) which stands for:

Brackets, Indices (or Order,) Division, Multiplication, Addition and Subtraction.

This tells you the order in which to complete mathematical questions. First complete any brackets, then powers, division, multiplication, addition and finally subtraction.

I didn't use this example to make those who got the answer right feel superior but to show how mistakes are commonly made even in straightforward mathematics, and how this can lead to pointless debates.

For a subject that is compulsory at school, it is a real shame that these stupid debates are taking place.

So why does this happen?

I believe one answer is boredom.

For a subject as important as mathematics, which is used as an IQ signpost by schools and employers in selection stages, and continuously linked to perceived mental abilities as children grow up, there's a surprising lack of real-world examples of the subject provided in class.

Let me set the scene. Imagine yourself back in a Maths classroom about to start a typical lesson.

'Today we are going to learn [insert mathematical concept here],' says your teacher. 'We'll start by listening to me drone on about [said concept], doing a few examples as a class then completing an endless list of practice questions until you can repeat [said concept] in an exam setting.'

Does this sound familiar?

No wonder Maths is often seen as a dry or boring subject. But imagine, for a moment, if the following scene occurred:

'Have you ever wondered why it seems like buses always come in threes?[5],' says the teacher. 'Or how likely it is for a critical hit to occur in this game? Or how this magic trick works? Well, today we are going to answer these questions by learning some statistics.'

Doesn't this lesson immediately sound more exciting?

Not only would students learn a concept, they'd immediately be able to apply it to solve an interesting problem and would leave lessons able to explain a real-world situation.

Exam preparation shouldn't be the only reason behind learning.

If you were lucky, your teacher knew this and turned to competitive games and puzzles to motivate you to learn a new concept.

Though there is an option of Functional Skills exams for English and Maths instead of a GCSE, which covers real-world applications for these subjects, these are quite unpopular by schools. The exam board OCR, which used to provide Functional Skills exams, decided to withdraw from providing these qualifications from September 2020[6]. (I hadn't heard about these exams until a friend mentioned them to me, but it sounds like a loss to the kind of learning I'd like to see taking place in schools.)

Key Point #4: Maths calculations aren't just about numbers – they require logic too

Maths is one of the few subjects in which the answers given by students tend to be either 'wrong' or 'right'.

I would argue, however, that this can lead to a tendency for both teachers and students to become stuck to a model of rote learning that fails to encourage other types of thinking when solving Maths problems.

Let me present myself (at the young age of 11) as Exhibit A in the first of three examples to illustrate my point.

Exam paper:
> Question: 'What is the average height of a woman?'
> Answer options: 0.5m 1m 1.5m 2m 2.5m 3m 4m

Looked at logically, the answer is obvious: it's 1.5m. (The actual figure according to a quick Google search is 1.64m for the UK[7].)

When I answered the question under exam pressure, however, I saw the word 'average', and instantly went to the number in the middle. This led me to circle 2m.

I didn't do this because I'm stupid, but because I hadn't applied a real-world checker to my calculations as I was barrelling through the paper at speed.

Has something similar ever happened to you?

I asked my nine-year-old brother (let's call him Exhibit B) the following question:

> 'You're driving a train on the London Underground. There are eight carriages on the train. On the first stop seven people enter each carriage. The train leaves the station. How old is the train driver?'

He said the answer was eight as there were eight carriages on the train. Did you get the answer right?

This is a classic example of a question which contains numbers and 'presents' itself as Maths, but the numbers in the question are red herrings and completely irrelevant to the actual question being asked. 'YOU are driving a train…' is the real clue to the correct answer. When I asked my brother, the answer should've been nine as he is nine years old.

So yes, it's a trick question. And yes, you might argue it's one that children are more likely to fall for than adults (though I've seen plenty of adults get it wrong too – try it yourself and see).

However, it comes with a valuable lesson in thinking logically before answering any question, even ones that we have been trained to see in numbers before anything else.

Sometimes both Maths skills and logic are required, as the following example (aka Exhibit C) illustrates:

A TV and a DVD player are on sale and have a total cost of £750. The TV costs £500 more than the DVD player. How much does the DVD player cost?

Did you immediately think of £250? That's your initial reaction because you do £750 – £500 in your head. However, if you think about this answer, you'll realise it's incorrect.

The real answer – and congratulations if you got this – is £125 (solved by thinking of two algebraic equations: $x + y = £750$ and $x - y = £500$).

Again the 'trick' here is not thinking about the question clearly enough before rushing in to provide an answer. Maths isn't just a series of equations; an application of logic is sometimes required too.

Essay-based subjects with discursive writing, discussing morals, philosophy and more, all come with the suggestion of choice – and with it the requirement to analyse a question/decision before jumping to a conclusion/deciding an answer.

Wouldn't it be good to consider the value of this in ALL subjects taught at school, even the ones with so-called 'right' and 'wrong' answers such as Maths?

The next time you see a mathematical question, take an opportunity to process logically what the question is asking for before you start your calculation. You might be surprised by the different method and solution that presents itself.

Key Point #5: A good knowledge of statistics allows you to critically analyse data

Statistical analysis is an underrated skill. They are vital to show comparisons and quickly illustrate points. For example:

According to a report by the Education Policy Institute from August 2018, in areas outside of London, just over a third (37%) of Maths teachers in the poorest schools had a relevant degree. Only 50% of Maths (and Physics) teachers in government schools stayed on for longer than five years[8].

Statistics are vital in showing comparisons and for quickly illustrating points such as the one above. It is easy to be shocked from this data that around two thirds of Maths teachers in deprived areas of the UK, outside of London, do not have a relevant degree – even though they are teaching students mathematics in preparation for examinations. This highlights a key disparity in the quality of teaching in schools across the UK.

Not all interpretations are this straightforward.

The phrase, 'correlation does not mean causation' is written in the syllabus as a learning point in Year 11, the year of GCSE exams. A well-known example of this is the off-cited claim that the length of women's skirts correlated with the rise and fall of the stock market in the 1920s[9].

The media often uses statistics to prove a general claim. It's quite common, for example, to read a variation on the claim that a study somewhere suggests that the number of takeaways ordered per night positively correlates with cancer rates in that place. Away from the headline, however, there are clearly other factors at play – people who order takeaways regularly are less likely to be active and thus are more likely to already be obese or unhealthy, for example, which are risk factors for cancer in themselves.

Or that a significant number of people in the study were also heavy smokers, which also elevates an individual's risk of the disease.

So while yes, technically, the above study could be taken as a correlative study, in this case the causative effect is explained through scientific interpretation rather than a direct extrapolation from the data.

Either way, closer examination of the individuals who took part in this 'study' would be required before coming to any concrete conclusions.

Wouldn't some analysis behind the statistics of a headline be useful to study in schools?

Even the most basic analyses performed on a set of data can provide a wealth of information into the accuracy of a certain test as well as providing aesthetic ways to present data, which can be important for many presentations in future life.

The skill arises from choosing a correct test to evaluate the data and being able to explain your rationale, as shown below for the context of a school examination:

- Mode: provides nominal data which is less effected by extreme values.

- Mean: helpful to determine which students are above or below average.
- Median and IQR: The interquartile range (determined from calculating Q3 – Q1 where Q3 is the 'median' of the top half and Q1 is the 'median' of the lower half,) is useful to differentiating cohorts and then creating class sets based on ability.

This test data can then be further manipulated, by separating the results from different groups and comparing the means and medians of each. Groups for comparison might be:

- Boys vs Girls
- Students of one teacher vs another teacher
- Students going on to A-level Maths vs those dropping Maths

Interesting real-world questions can then be answered by using statistical analysis.

Top independent schools and universities are constantly being scrutinised for their racial and class distribution of intake. Statistics provide one way to easily analyse the composition of different institutions or different years at the same institution providing an invaluable reference point for the comparison of various datasets.

However, this statistical data can be easily altered and skewed to support a particular outcome, and as such, care should be taken when presented with statistics.

Every day we're bombarded with statistical claims and data that, much like the statement below, present themselves as 'fact':

46.4% of all published statistics are false.

Really?

No. I just made that up.

Unfortunately, these are found everywhere, including (or should that be 'especially') on social media platforms.

However convenient it may be to accept statistics at face-value, this can hide the bad data analysis that was performed to obtain the figure.

A statement such as 75% of all children at a certain school have ginger hair may seem extraordinary until you find out that the school is based in Scotland and the sample size was four.

You might see a beauty advert on TV which says at the bottom of the screen '82% of 60 women agreed their hair looks brighter'. Upon examination of the published test results it's revealed that the results were 'based on a survey of 100 women'.

This is a classic example of 'cherry-picking' data or sampling bias: the 60 women were cherry-picked from the 100 total women who took part. If you repeated the analysis on the original 100, you'll see it's really 49% of women who agreed their hair looked brighter. Which is less than half.

In 2007, the toothpaste company Colgate was ordered to remove its claim that 'More than 80% of dentists recommend Colgate' by the Advertising Standards Authority (ASA) after it was revealed the dentists could choose more than one toothpaste brand and that a competitor's brand was chosen by the dentists almost as frequently as Colgate (but never mentioned).

Even governments publish misleading statistics.

Throughout March 2020, the UK government-announced daily death toll for Covid-19 was revealed to be a much lower number than the true figure, with more than 40% (around 670) of actual deaths unaccounted for[10] – something that could be partly explained when we learn that the deaths included in those figures were only those that occurred in hospitals and up until 5pm on any given day.

These are but a handful of examples of where a given claim from a statistical test or analysis may appear to be supported at first glance, but upon careful examination warrants further questioning into their reliability, accuracy and chosen method.

Wouldn't a better understanding of how to question information allow us to better interpret and draw our own conclusions rather than blindly accept what an 'expert', the media, or anyone else is telling us to be correct?

Recommended reading

The following books are a great introduction to the hidden application of real-world mathematics (Wyndham) and the impact of rare and unpredictable events (Taleb).

Why Do Buses Come in Threes? – Jeremy Wyndham
Black Swan – Nicholas Taleb

ENGLISH

English. The very language this book is written in. One that's spoken on six continents and serves as an official language in over 70 countries.

Modern English as we know it today is a mixture of Germanic Old English, French- and Latin-influenced Middle English, and many foreign words adapted from Britain's colonisation of and influence upon other countries.

And English is constantly evolving. From text-speak to memes, the way we communicate with each other is changing rapidly.

English is a compulsory subject in schools in the UK until the age of 16. Two English GCSEs are sat – one in English Language and one in English Literature.

Like Maths, English is a compulsory subject precisely because of its importance as the foundation of other subjects and life-skills.

Surely, therefore, being able to read and write competently should be the first priority for schools?

Key Point #1a: The levels of illiteracy in UK children is worryingly high

In 2016, the Royal Literary Trust reported that 16.4% of adults in the UK (around seven million people) had 'very poor literacy skills'[1]. This figure is strikingly similar to a report by the OECD in 2015 that reported 18% of 15 year olds in England and Scotland failed to have a minimum level of reading proficiency[2].

What is happening here? Why are a significant proportion of students failing to score the 'required grades' in formal examinations or leaving school with a basic understanding of literacy in a subject compulsory for their education?

The children who miss the government targets are often from disadvantaged backgrounds in deprived areas. By stopping short of these initial milestones, these students become less likely to hit future government progress guidelines at KS3 and above.

You might ask whether this problem has arisen due to lack of learning opportunities in the home and at school for these children or from the curriculum.

That would be a very good question. The curriculum is certainly a blanket one-size-fits-all approach, which provides a uniform level of education to every student.

But it makes little difference if a class is assigned books to read from a set list of English 20th-century authors if some
students in that class can't read at all.

Key Point #1b: The abundance of common mistakes in basic English across the population is all too easily overlooked

According to the Royal Literary Trust, in 2018, 64% of students achieved a good grade in English language GCSE or equivalent (grades A*-C or Level 9-4)[3].

Which is great, right?

So why are there still so many mistakes made in common words and phrases?

Could technology and the increasing reliance on auto-correct be accelerating illiteracy rates?

Scrolling through social media channels, it is easy to find many instances of basic grammatical errors.

Some common examples are listed below:

- They're vs Their vs There
- Complimentary (free/giving a complement) vs Complementary (goes with)
- Affect (verb) vs Effect (noun)
- Person X and me vs Person X and I
- Lose (to no longer have something) vs Loose (not tight)
- Assure (remove someone's doubts) vs Insure (protect) vs Ensure (guarantee)
- Less vs Fewer (supermarkets really should put 10 items or 'fewer'!)
- Then (adverb) vs Than (conjunction for comparisons)
- Your (belonging to you) vs You're (you are)

The list goes on and on…

Mistakes don't only occur in grammar. Phrases are also prone to the muddled-up treatment. Here a few examples of some interesting variations and the phrases they came from:

- *'Escape goat'* – Scapegoat
- *'Right from the gecko'* – Right from the get-go
- *'From all intensive purposes'* – From all intents and purposes
- *'Biting my time'* – Biding my time
- *'Piece of mind'* – Peace of mind
- *'Could of'* – Could have

- *'Free reign'* – Free rein
- *'Mute point'* – Moot point

Again, there are many more (some of my favourites of which are highlighted by Dave Gorman in his PowerPoint-based comedy shows).

Now I acknowledge that we've all made mistakes in our use of English, sometimes knowingly and sometimes unknowingly. I'm sure the editor of the first (and second) draft of this book found many.

It's also true that some 'mistakes' become so widely used they in turn become part of the ever-evolving language and those new meanings make their way into dictionaries over time. (The word syllabus, for example, was actually a misreading of the Ancient Greek word '*sittybos*' which meant a table of contents.)

But while an incorrect version of English may lead to nothing more than ridicule on social media, this becomes more worrying when it occurs in emails, letters and official documents. The occasional error that can change the meaning of a sentence/phrase is embarrassing enough without the added hazard of unknowingly using words and phrases you believe to be correct.

This could be detrimental if it occurs in a personal statement for an application or when reaching out to a prospective new client.

The written English that you choose to use in a given situation, such as in an email, could significantly impact the first impression that you present of yourself.

Therefore, schools should ensure that ALL students leave school with solid literacy skills that will enable them to communicate effectively with a diverse array of people, from friends and peers all the way to CEOs.

Key Point #2: The current English curriculum rewards rote-learning set ideas and themes of books rather than encouraging independent analysis

English Literature, as it is currently taught in schools, suffers from one vital flaw: it is highly subjective.

On one side is the author's original opinion and message, whether conveyed outright or in more subtle means (either consciously or in some cases unconsciously).

Then there's the opinion of the teacher or reader who's conveying the message they believe is being stated by the author – or what has become the 'received wisdom' of an author's intention.

In the current school curriculum, rather than inviting less conventional interpretations of an author's work, students habitually learn the opinions of their teacher. When they mention these in a piece of homework, they get marks as the teacher agrees with his/her own analysis, and the student's belief that the teacher's insight is the 'right' one is reinforced by their high mark.

Is it up to the author to explicitly state what he/she means? Or for the reader to come up with their own ideas and theories about the text? What if the author changes his/her mind? Or if the reader is applying a subconscious level of bias to their analysis and 'begins to twist facts to suit theories, instead of theories to suit facts'[4] as Sherlock Holmes notes in *A Scandal in Bohemia*?

Any piece of fiction can be interpreted in multiple ways that lead to very interesting discussions.

A well-known example of how these views may not align is illustrated in the 'blue curtains' literary critique, which I've paraphrased below:

The teacher reads the line 'The curtains are blue' to mean that the blue represents the sad and melancholy environment. The author meant, 'The curtains are f***ing blue.'

When it comes to a creative work of fiction, who's to say what is or isn't correct?

But rather than explore and celebrate the possibilities of this, I believe the scope for individual thinking becomes more limited the more a certain work has been analysed at school and its ideas become 'set'. These include works by Shakespeare (*Hamlet, Othello, Twelfth Night, Romeo and Juliet*), Dickens (*Great Expectations, A Christmas Carol*), HG Wells (*War of the Worlds*), Jane Austen (*Pride and Prejudice*) and Mark Hadden (*Curious Incident of the Dog in the Night-time*) – all of which are listed on the website SparkNotes alongside their key themes (with examples).

If you can memorise interpretations and themes for an exam, there's no need to think. Suddenly the disconnect between the subjective nature of markers and the content that you write becomes glaringly apparent.

Instead of the so-called critical thinking and analysis that an English classroom is theoretically supposed to cultivate, the process of preparing for exams – at least at GCSE level – contains more rote-learning than anything else.

Indeed, there's a sort of 'quote culture' taught in schools in which students spend their revision time memorising points and quotes and then write paraphrased explanations from their English teachers. It's known as:

How to PEE.

Yes, this is a real concept (stop sniggering!) and stands for:

- Point
- Evidence (the quote)
- Explanation

Learning yes, understanding no.

For Great Expectations I was taught that Estella's name comprised of 'e' and 'stella' which means far away and star. As a faraway star, Estella was out of Pip's reach. I thought this was an over analysis of Dickens' text, but did I mention it in my exam? You bet; I wanted the marks.

Or what if, on the other hand, your teacher does have a slightly unorthodox perspective and is keen to share it – only for the examiner to disagree (most likely because it is different from the common interpretations of the text)?

What if your teacher thought that the character of Scrooge and his development in the story was a representation of Dickens' own changing views towards Christmas, say, when more likely theories are that Scrooge was based on the miser John Elwes[5] with his views on the poor from the economist Thomas Malthus[6]?

There's a good chance you'd be awarded a lower mark because it's an unconventional interpretation and then feel upset with your achievement, even though you put in the effort to memorise your teacher's explanations.

Therefore, while less original thoughts and perspectives are preferred, using them is still a risky approach in the current school model.

But if students have an unconventional idea or perspective, wouldn't it be better for them to feel able to discuss them in the classroom? And if they can evidence from use of the text, shouldn't they be encouraged to have strength in their convictions, rather than conforming to those of their teacher?

I believe independent thinking inspires passion and drive, which are essential skills to reach levels that others are unable to or are too scared to climb.

The beauty of literature is that it is so open to interpretation. Shouldn't this be better explored in schools?

Key Point #3: English literary analysis should incorporate more themes of race and sexuality to balance modern 21st century beliefs with those of the past

There are very few themes or ideas exploring race, culture, gender or sexuality in the current English curriculum, especially at GCSE level when book choices become restricted by an exam syllabus.

With LGBT and racial themes more widely explored in the 21st century, more acceptance of LGBT people and an understanding of the complexities of the issues surrounding racial discrimination becoming more widespread, shouldn't the curriculum be updated to reflect the full diversity of the world today's students are going into?

According to the GOV.UK website, studying GCSE English Literature requires works from the following categories[7]:

- At least one play by Shakespeare
- At least one 19th century novel
- Poetry from after 1789, including representative Romantic poetry
- Fiction or drama from the British Isles from 1914 onwards.

As a result of the impact of Covid-19, Ofqual announced in August 2020 that students sitting the English Literature exam in 2021 will only need to choose two topics from the last three in the list, further limiting the scope of English covered in the classroom[8].

There are some notable works of fiction that explore the above. Racism is a primary theme in Harper Lee's *To Kill a Mockingbird* (1960), for example, and the book is routinely studied in the US school curriculum and, to a lesser extent, in schools in the UK.

However, 'To Kill A Mockingbird' no longer fits any of the GCSE English Literature criteria listed.

In May 2014, Michael Gove removed this book along with *Of Mice and Men* (John Steinbeck) from the syllabus in favour of putting 'English [authors]' back into 'English Literature'. (Some online reports even claim the books were removed because Michael Gove didn't like them[9].)

So, while schools are of course still able to study these books, they're no longer compulsory to read or able to be used in examinations. They're likely, therefore, to appear on fewer and fewer syllabuses.

According to Stonewall, the government announced new regulations in April 2019 for teaching Relationships and Sex Education in England, to come into effect in September 2020[10], that will add LGBT relationships to Sex Education classes and PSHE.

This is a great first step, but why stop there? Why not touch upon the theme in other subjects, such as English and History? (Incorporating them into the GCSE syllabus when children are 15-16, should be less of an issue to those parents who object to their young children learning about LGBT themes.)

So, are there any alternatives that might fit instead? *Maurice*, by E.M. Forster fits the criteria outlined for GCSE. It tells the story of a working-class homosexual man who interacts with the upper-to-middle classes and falls in love while exposing their privileges. As such this book offers plenty of opportunities to explore themes around sexuality as well as class.

And this is merely an example. LGBT themes in 'classic' literature may be relatively rare, but they're not as rare as their lack of exposure on the current English syllabus might suggest. This would provide a great starting point for discussion and widening the scope around the theme of romance in English literature.

And why not also take a wider look at the authors themselves, where relevant, to offer inspiration?

In the early 19th century, for example, there was a young man who couldn't attend school and whose father was in jail. He had little confidence he could write and many of his initial stories were rejected. It was only when he received his first positive feedback among the many rejections that he began to write more and become the author we still read today.

His name? Charles Dickens.

Wouldn't that inspire you as a student?

Teachers and schools may of course choose to use their own books to fill this void, but if a book isn't compulsory, like *To Kill A Mockingbird*, they're much less likely to do so.

A wider approach to diversity in English would also open discussions that could reduce bullying rates based on the misconceptions of certain minorities and would create a more inclusive school environment. This would be more representative of a world we would want to live in.

Key Point #4: The English curriculum is too restricted and outdated to prepare students for their future aspirations in the ever-changing 21st century

The English Language GCSE is different from its Literature counterpart in that it normally requires some sort of comprehension followed by an original piece of writing.

In this section, the quality of analysis is marked for the comprehension, with some early marks requiring a portion of 'copy and paste' from the text. In the latter half – the creative writing – students have more freedom to use their imagination and utilise their improved knowledge of vocabulary, grammar and writing styles.

At school, free writing in the form of letters of complaint, poems, plays, and in the style of certain authors are also practised to give students an excellent opportunity to apply their creativity.

Which is great. But what if the English Language curriculum also had more real-world applications? Mightn't it be useful to write a formal letter of complaint or a cover letter for a future job application or similar as part of the English Language GCSE?

For the comprehension part, what if the set-text was a current news article instead of a work of fiction? This would help students to build skills with real-life applications outside school, such as being able to critically analyse reports and identify incongruencies in English grammar. At A-level, works of parody and of a satirical nature are studied, alongside other analyses of journalism and media-linked reports. Perhaps some of these topics and even the changing nature of how literature is absorbed, from books to ebooks and beyond, could be discussed in GCSE English?

Another option might be to analyse a few basic texts from other academic subjects, including STEM or Law texts, with a greater focus on the structuring and writing style than the content. This could greatly improve the writing capabilities of future students who underestimate the amount of essay writing involved in their subject in university and beyond.

Other options might include the following:

- The analysis of terms and conditions of documents or contracts
- Looking at uses of English to persuade in marketing and in legal courtrooms
- How to negotiate effectively

Collectively, this would integrate the core concept of literacy and illustrate real-world examples of its uses in more generalised purposes.

Encouraging students to read around topics they're interested in will increase their knowledge in those fields and offset boredom.

Even if the proportion of students who are failing to reach the government required grade at GCSE remains the same, at least those students will have been given some practical guidance in written English to take with them into later life.

SPORT

Sport has earned its place here because it's a fundamental 'subject' timetabled in schools across all ages from primary school to secondary school.

Known as 'Games' in some schools, at least one afternoon of the weekly timetable is dedicated to sport throughout a student's academic journey.

Why is it so important?

Reports have continuously stated links between regular exercise helping to improve the academic performance of students[1], as well as increasing mental resilience[2] and decreasing the likelihood of mental illnesses[3].

Exercise is important on its own, but Sport also encourages students to try out different activities, requires practice to improve and is one of the few activities at school with an emphasis on teamwork.

However, I believe it could do more.

Key Point #1: In order to maximise the benefits of all sports at school, students should be given a basic knowledge of how to perform techniques correctly to avoid injuries

If you enter a physiotherapist's office, what would you see?

You'll likely find the walls lined with posters of various muscle groups detailing their functions and the ways they can be injured or over-stretched.

Now, you don't need that level of information to enjoy Sport and participate in it safely but some knowledge of muscle function and basic anatomy is very useful to know.

Did you know, for example, that many personal trainers recommend working out larger muscle groups first before working the smaller groups, e.g. lats before rhomboids? Or that a bad back can be caused by a weak core which both leads to and is caused by bad posture, forcing the lower back muscles to overcompensate and causing that aforementioned pain?

Instead of shouting from across the room to complete 20 press-ups as so many students will be familiar with from school, wouldn't it better for a teacher to encourage their students in correct technique, stop students who aren't capable of 'dropping and doing 20' to perform fewer or modified press-ups?

Think about it. If you were in a Maths class a teacher would immediately spot if you were using the wrong method in your practice questions after showing examples to the class. You wouldn't be told to get on and finish your work; instead you'd be reminded of the correct technique and be expected to show how you would correctly apply it before advancing onto other situations and harder questions.

Performing a technique correctly is more important than any number – it helps prevent injuries, instils a good practice and ensures the right muscle groups are being put to use. The weight used can be slowly increased over time once these foundations are in place.

In Sport, technique is more important than power or speed. The 'mistakes' that result from incorrect technique won't just inhibit both of those, they can lead to short and long-term injuries.

Key Point #2: All students should be encouraged and motivated to improve – especially those who aren't 'natural' athletes

For me, this is personal.

Let me explain.

In my teenage years I was one of the weakest students in my all-boys cohort. One or two PE teachers even called me weak for having a skinny build and focused their efforts on the stronger members of the class. This may have been one of the reasons why I was regularly picked last for Sport teams.

This led me down the classic path for those who wish to defend themselves and prevent physical altercations without the need for brute force: martial arts.

I became sick and tired of the martial arts coaches who were teaching ineffective methods and told me that I couldn't yet do or learn a certain skill. I was determined to know how I could quickly and effectively stand my ground against people who thought I was small and fragile.

So I started to look for coaches who said I could and were willing to teach me how. And guess what? I found them.

These coaches encouraged me to start going to the gym and showed me how to punch harder and faster. They were the ones that made me realise that motivation and the correct basic know-how will allow anybody to achieve their goals and that you need them both or else it becomes very difficult to progress. Yes, I had a smaller and skinnier build, but with their help, I became motivated to work harder than everyone else, which built up my mental resilience and competitive strive.

Now, I know that the gym has a reputation as a competitive, toxic, masculine-focused environment. And yes, there are plenty of people who seem to use them solely for the benefit of posting narcissistic images on their social media feeds and bragging to the mates about the heaviest weight they can deadlift.

But as someone who's learned first-hand how much benefit can be gained from following the methods and advice of the right trainer at the gym, my advice is to ignore these self-absorbed people. There's a lot to be gained by doing so.

Whenever my posture could be improved in a class or session, my Personal Trainers/coaches were quick to help me adopt the correct position without demoralising my efforts. They alerted me to the importance of a proper warm-up and cool down before training and the benefits they provided by reducing my risk of injury.

I am grateful for these inspiring coaches and personal trainers who built up my confidence and abilities while simultaneously teaching me amazing techniques and methods that I continue to use. They have increased my mental resilience and have empowered me in my drive and determination for future projects and ambitions.

Looking back, I wonder why this same attitude and advice wasn't given by my PE teachers at school.

There are football coaches, PE instructors, volleyball referees and whole range of roles for teachers and staff to help students improve, encourage good sportsmanship and mediate any disputes.

But where are the ones who motivate you to improve?

My experience has given me the belief that everyone can find a sport that they can enjoy and build a passion for. But you need encouragement and motivation to do that.

An easy way for school Sports lessons to improve would be to place a greater emphasis on individual student's growth and achievements rather than comparing students to each other, and to ensure that all students have the encouragement they require to excel in their chosen sport.

Sports awards are a common method used to share successes with other people. The simple idea of wearing the same coloured shirt as those in the same house, club, group etc… can provide a sense of team pride.

Students should be made to feel proud of all their sporting accomplishments regardless of whether or not they're recognised by others, and to strive for continuous personal development to reach their goals.

Key Point #3: Nutrition is just as important as exercise in order to maintain a healthy lifestyle and to change your body's physique if desired

If you pass any primary school during break-time, chances are you'll see or hear children playing outside, enjoying themselves as they chase each other around the playground.

Sports should be – and are – fun!

As outlined in the previous point, motivation is a huge limiting factor in this. Combine it with a poor 'health literacy', however, and this becomes a recipe for disaster.

The NHS estimates the levels of obesity in UK adults to be around one in four people[4]. Office jobs or remote working that are almost entirely composed of sitting at a desk don't help. The government created the 'Couch to 5K' plan to encourage exercise. But sport and exercise need to be supported with good nutrition.

There's a phrase you might have heard of that states 'abs are made in the kitchen'.

Its point, of course, is to illustrate the vital role of diet and nutrition in our physical wellbeing. So why is this barely touched on at school?

School lunches have become considerably healthier over the past decade, with limits placed on many fatty and sugary foods, and more vegetarian/vegan and healthy options added to menus. However, this fails to combat the problem of what students eat outside of school, even with the government's introduction of a sugar tax.

If students were better informed about nutrition, they'd be able to make better choices for themselves with regard to what they eat – both at school and at home.

Your body is bound by the laws of thermodynamics; energy cannot be created nor destroyed. Similarly, all these diet plans that suggest that you should not eat after 8pm, avoid carbs (ketogenic diet), avoid meat (vegetarian), fast for the majority of the day (intermittent fasting) etc. may work because they compel you to eat fewer calories, but they do NOT work because of some trick that hacks your metabolism into a fat-burning mode, as is often suggested.

Therefore, exercise is not the sole factor crucial to a healthy lifestyle or in building muscle mass or losing fat. Was this ever mentioned in PE?

I believe even a small focus on nutrition could be enormously useful in helping students navigate what can, at times, feel like increasingly complex and contradictory dietary advice (for those who are interested to know more, I have included a short 'Nutrition Guide' as an Appendix to this book).

Exercise is important, but it's not the only important factor when it comes to maintaining a healthy lifestyle or in building muscle mass or losing fat. Was this ever mentioned in PE?

GCSES

HUMANITIES

GEOGRAPHY

A subject that literally covers the entire globe. The exact definition of what 'is' Geography is constantly being altered and updated. Geography is a massive subject and can be split into two over-arching subsections, Human and Physical.

Physical Geography covers the Earth's climate, rocks, landforms, volcanoes, earthquakes, rivers, erosion and other natural phenomena. Human Geography observes the topics of tourism, the development of countries and major cities, urban and rural environments, globalisation, trade, population and migration.

As with most subjects in the UK curriculum, Geography tends to focus on Britain as one of its main topics. Many schools and universities run Geography field trips in the UK to keep costs (and the trip's carbon footprint) low, and to enable the majority of students to take part. This provides a great opportunity for students to explore more of the country that they live in, and understand the important difference between the UK, England and Great Britain.

Geography teaching also covers a lot of interesting and important global topics: the latitudes of deserts and tropics and the climates of the seven continents. However, this raises the question on why some adults have such a lack of knowledge in basic global geography in the UK and elsewhere.

Watching videos of members of the general public online unable to correctly identify Australia or Middle Eastern countries (Iran/Iraq/Afghanistan) on a map might be amusing. But it also highlights a real problem that develops when Geography teaching is absent or forgotten. After all, how can people feel and express cultural sensitivity towards a place and its people when they don't even know where it is?

Key Point #1: Geography shows the increasing importance of how we impact the world around us

In the 21st century when Geography-related issues are in the headlines almost daily, why is the subject not compulsory to take to GCSE like the Sciences?

One major concern covered in Geography at school that is gaining increased awareness due to the efforts of people such as Greta Thunberg and organisations including Extinction Rebellion (though some of their chosen methods and actions warrant some questioning,) is the effect of global warming.

Global warming affects us all because it is increasing the temperature of the very planet we require to survive.

It's all too easy to get lost in the debate over whether global warming is a problem of our own making. However, I believe that this makes the situation seem too vague and impersonal.

Regardless of whether you believe it to be a man-made or natural phenomenon, or even a mix of both, we all leave behind a carbon footprint on the world around us. More specifically the beneficial measures that we already know we could take – issues such as ensuring that there is a balance between nature and infrastructure in our cities and towns, and making industrial production cleaner by decreasing emissions of toxic gases – should be compulsory learning in schools.

The lockdowns imposed by the Covid-19 pandemic had the sudden effect of reducing levels of transport, both local and global, as well as causing reductions in industrial operations to a greater extent that could have been achieved by environmental campaigners. Levels of the toxic gas carbon monoxide (CO) dropped by 50% in New York during the lockdown in March 2020 compared to March 2019, while there were worldwide reductions in CO_2 emissions when factories were temporarily shut down[1].

Even though Covid-19 has been a devastating global pandemic, it may well provide a 'green lining' by increasing everybody's awareness of the environment. By being more informed about the benefits of reduced greenhouse gas emissions, these reduced levels could be sustained, or at the very least not brought back up to what they were before. It will be up to us – as individuals, companies and governments – whether we return to our usual levels of pollution or continue the trend towards a greener lifestyle.

However, environmental sustainability isn't just about managing global warming – it's also about reducing pollution and waste.

Sustainable investing, recycling, carbon-neutral products and electric cars are a few examples of methods being used to save the planet and make our society more sustainable. But the rate that this is advancing could be too slow.

In London, levels of air pollution may look to be decreasing: the average roadside level of nitrogen dioxide (NO_2) decreased from 44.3 to 36.2 µg/m³ between August 2017 to August 2019, but upon examination of the data from this 24 month period, data recorded for 19 of these months (79%) had levels over the

EU legal limit of 40μg/m^3 [2]. In this way, it's important to support learning about environmental issues with concrete, recent data, and then apply that data in a specific context.

This could be one potential solution to increasing the Geography knowledge of the general population so that they have an understanding of the important issues of global warming (and can make their own informed decision as to its cause,) while being aware of the changes occurring on the very planet we pass on to future generations.

Key Point #2: Applying the knowledge covered in the broad subject of Geography to real-world examples and relatable actions has the potential to lead to real difference

Geography is a very broad subject with its composition an amalgamation of aspects from Politics, Economics, History, Philosophy, Biology, Psychology, and Geology.

Geography at all levels combines various ideologies and concepts from these subjects.

Imagine the impact on the future environment that could be achieved by encouraging students to come up with ways to apply their new knowledge in sustainability and conservation to their everyday lives – instead of simply remembering methods to mention in a field trip or exam.

For example, a few of the students I spoke to over the course of my research for this book had undertaken field trips to Newham or Tower Hamlets – two of London's poorest boroughs – as part of their analysis of the distribution of social housing and levels of crime across London. Walking around those areas to collect data from checklists and surveys was, they reported, both interactive and eye-opening. Recognising the effects of 'white flight', the displacement effect of gentrification and population density are indeed key points of consideration.

But what about asking more in-depth questions? Are rates of crime, violence and recidivism high in these areas because youths are bored and so become involved in gangs? Or perhaps they believe that being in a gang is necessary to protect themselves from other gangs in neighbouring areas? Are arrest rates higher because of a racial bias in stop and search rates? Are wages low because few businesses want to have branches in deprived areas and because they would prefer to have a certain 'clientele'? Is gentrification so prominent because land in these areas is cheap for investors to purchase and build on? Or is the land particularly bad for building on due to its poor foundations and connections to transport links?

The above highlights some very basic connections between behavioural economics, human geography, social studies, psychology and physical geography, just from looking at one case study. So why aren't political and social theorists and their writings also on the A-level Geography curriculum?

Indeed, the premise of looking at individual case studies in a 'vacuum' and splitting Human and Physical Geography could also be a reason for the poor understanding of the overarching composition of the subject as a whole – something that currently only begins to be analysed in Geography at university level.

A GCSE student may know all the statistics concerning tourism numbers in Blackpool in a given year or the types of rocks and terrain found in the UK but fail to make the connection between the Human and Physical Geography they've learned. In this case, Blackpool has a low-level terrain which is a risk-factor towards flooding. Therefore, the local council started a series of improvements to the promenade and the construction of a new sea wall to mitigate any adverse effects to the locals, tourists and finances of the seaside town.

The beauty of having so many different subjects make up Geography allows for fascinating links to be made between them and for insightful discussions that can pull from all the subjects simultaneously. Unfortunately, this rarely occurs in Geography classrooms at school. These links might help students analyse processes over space and time rather than single case studies.

Geography students have the best chance of implementing change if they learn not just the contemporary buzzwords and issues, but also develop the theoretical frameworks in order to analyse new knowledge in a socially responsible way. More emphasis could be placed on applying knowledge to real-world situations rather than being directed at obtaining marks. Case studies of a given location in higher education (A-levels and university) could involve real contact with people from that area and the composition of a series of (hypothetical) action plans that could be taken to mitigate a certain issue.

In this way, exams could contain more analysis of potential solutions to a given situation rather than listing the problems. The longer essay-based questions could require links to be made from all aspects of Geography, with a stronger emphasis on students choosing their own factors and avenues of consideration, and being able to explain their rationale when tackling a complex problem.

Recommended reading

The following books provide further insights into Geography not currently covered in the classroom, and its applications to real problems in the wider world.

Geography – Danny Dorling & Carl Lee
International Migration: A Very Short Introduction – Khalid Koser
Hazards – Malcolm Skinner
The Invention of Nature – Andre Wulf

HISTORY

Mark Twain's alleged take on the subject is that 'History never repeats itself but it often rhymes'. This is an interesting interpretation of the cliché that events in our history repeat themselves, but each 'repetition' has the same overall pattern with subtle differences.

History is often taught from as early as primary-school and remains compulsory up to the age of 14. In the UK, the focus leans heavily towards British history at GCSE level[1]. Up to that point, schools have the flexibility to teach any period of history. But from GCSE, the curriculum follows stricter guidelines.

Let's start our romp through the past with a very basic question. How do we begin to build our knowledge about History? Whatever the time period, how would you expect to find the information you require? Sources, of course. (And no, I'm not referring to the tomato kind.)

Key Point #1: Learning that's too focused on preparing to answer set exam questions and limited source material can narrow your perspective

Sources can be pictures, paintings, verbal or written accounts and in some rare cases artefacts and relics. These can hold a wealth of information about a certain event and are often used at school as evidence for the events that occurred during a certain time period – however all sources have an inherent flaw. They all have an initial purpose to convey some meaning, a message, an opinion. And as the interpretation of sources is subjective and opinions can change over time, a source only provides a snapshot of a situation at a specific moment in time.

I was told by my History teacher at school to 'question the question' as preparation for exam technique. The wider point of this was to realise if a question is asked about a certain period of History, why is this question being asked and does it have an implied answer that influences how you might answer the question? Is the question phrased in such a way as to guide you to a certain answer? For example:

'Through which methods did the Nazi regime use propaganda to indoctrinate its people?'

Does this sound familiar to you? Perhaps you learned a certain method such as the mnemonic below from the BBC Bitesize website[2], which suggests applying the following mnemonic to help recall the key features of Nazi propaganda:

- **Communication** - at the heart of propaganda
- **Should** - Sport
- **Remain** - Rallies
- **Really** - Radio
- **Positive** – Press

Based on that alone, however, and without a wider understanding of the facts you might believe that propaganda was all that was used to indoctrinate the German people. While we know propaganda was widely used, there were also other methods, such as terror, controlling the education system and maintaining absolute political control among others.

If you were sitting this question in an exam, you would be given a handful of select sources to analyse and guide you to an answer (or 'questioning the question', as that teacher of mine said). However, while you may not be required to mention these other methods in an exam setting, it doesn't make them any less important in understanding the wider issues surrounding the subject.

While this is a huge generalisation, Humanities subjects by their very nature tend to be more subjective than STEM subjects – and this applies to so-called 'fact-based' subjects such as History, too.

One interesting aspect of discussions (and arguments) in real-life with friends or members of the public is the vast array of information available that you could use as evidence for any points you make.

Keeping an open mind, tackling a question from several perspectives over time and even asking why the question is worded in the way that it is are all valuable points of critical thinking that are not always tackled in a classroom setting.

Relying on sources to offer a single, definitive 'proof' or answer a carefully worded question in a specific way may deliver the results you need to advance within the current school system, but it's an approach that's hugely limiting.

Key Point #2: History isn't just subjective – it's often written to support a victors' narrative that fails to acknowledge the multiple reasons and points of view behind the unfolding of events

You may have heard the line at school that 'History is written by the victors'. I'd take this one step further and state a more obvious claim: History is written by those who write the history books.

Due in some part to the subjectivity I mentioned previously, inaccurate or biased accounts of events have often found their way into History books – accounts that are then taught to the pupils studying the subject (who quite understandably have faith in the accuracy of the information they read in textbooks, written by 'expert' historians) as fact.

If I were to mention the Royal Air Force flying across Europe fighting the Germans in the 1940s, would you think of a British effort or a multinational force? When you think of the Enigma Code, do you think of Alan Turing or a team of international mathematicians? In both of these cases, the Poles played a significant contribution. In the Battle of Britain Polish pilots made up around 10% of the fighter pilot squad and it was the Polish mathematicians Marian Rejewski, Henryk Zygalski and Jerzy Różycki who provided Turing with crucial insights into mathematical codes and how to use electro-mechanical machines that put Turing on the path to cracking the code[3].

I'm not sharing this information to detract from the efforts of the British nor to bolster the efforts of the Poles, but rather to show that the 'history' we're taught is all too often presented as one-sided when there are likely to be multiple perspectives and many different stories that will have contributed to an event. All of which have the potential to enrich a student's knowledge and understanding.

Even if this interpretation wasn't required for an exam question, this doesn't mean that the understanding of the concept of there being more than one 'truth' isn't a useful life lesson for students.

Let's look at another example. The Spanish Armada.

In 1588, the Catholic King Philip II of Spain sent out over a hundred ships to try and invade England and remove the Protestant Queen Elizabeth I from the throne. The defeat of this so called 'Invincible Armada' by Sir Francis Drake, who managed to outmanoeuvre the enemy ships with a smaller fleet equipped with long range naval guns, was of course a great source of pride for the British.

It may seem that this battle was a win for the British, and that is the end of that.

However, as you have probably guessed by now, there's more to this story.

Some historians now argue that it was in fact poor weather – a strong south-westerly wind – that forced the Spanish fleet to retreat to the North Sea and which ultimately lost them the battle.

And for those of you who still think the English fleet's success was all down to Sir Francis Drake, let me refer you to the Anglo-Spanish War of 1589.

One year after the glorious defeat of the Spanish Armada, Drake decided to deploy another fleet, named the English Armada (or Counter Armada), to completely destroy Spain, but the entire effort was a complete disaster[4].

Did you learn about this at school?

I wouldn't be surprised if you hadn't. When Queen Elizabeth I heard about this catastrophe, she prohibited the publication of anything referring to this failed Counter Armada. While there is a lot of literature available for the Spanish Armada, there is far less for the Counter Armada and, as such, it has not been given the same attention[5].

Key Point #3: Behind every historical event are people – of different ethnicities, sexualities, genders, backgrounds and perspectives – all of whom should be considered in examining the mistakes of the past and applying this knowledge to the future

Depending on the exam board used you may have studied different periods of History – but I can almost guarantee that British History played a prominent role within the course.

British pride and victories are recurring themes when learning History at school.

Is the aim of this to raise school children who are patriotic and confident in their knowledge of the successes of British victories? What then of the uncomfortable truth that the British Empire was a source of great racial divides and left vast areas of Africa in poverty?

What do you mean, you didn't learn about that at school?

This is not an isolated example; most curricula around the world tend to be very country specific in what they teach.

In the early 16th century, the Spanish realised South America was full of precious metals including silver and gold. After initial expeditions to the Caribbean islands were expanded to nearby Central America, more and more Spanish conquistadors arrived in Central and South America on the hunt for Aztec and Incan precious metals.

This led to a long period of brutal exploitation in Central and South America, but for a long time this period was celebrated for Spain's success in 'conquering' these regions.

More recently, incidents such as the Cuban Missile Crisis or the Falklands War show that not all conflicts end in an easy win for the 'home' country. Often battles and wars are started through greed, a need to accumulate more resources, (the ongoing conflicts for oil in the Middle East, for example) or a way to expand and consolidate power.

For there to be 'victors', there must also be 'losers'. To maintain their influence, the 'victors' have to keep hold of their control.

Which brings me to another interesting question, if one of the purposes of History was to learn from the mistakes of the past, why does so much taught History focus on victories?

Neo-colonialism in Africa. The slave trades. The ongoing racism still prevalent in the world today. Have we really learned from history?

With the death of George Floyd by a white police officer at the end of May 2020, the outcry for Black History to be taught in schools, both in the US and the UK, has become more widespread.

This led to the toppling of statues of historical figures believed to have had roles in the slave trade. Arguments raged on both sides about whether History was being destroyed or rewritten in the process.

What I am raising here is not about whether these events should have happened, or all the reasons why they happened, but rather if a white-washed historical education system could be partly to blame.

While I support the Black Lives Matter movement, it's important to note there are many other members of society – and in the wider world – who receive little more than a passing mention in the school history books, both for their achievements and suppression.

My GCSE history teacher at school used to say: 'War is a catalyst of change'. And the reasons behind war can expose some hidden motivations rooted in discrimination.

The 19th century Belgian King Leopold II was responsible for the deaths of around 10 million Africans in Congo in acts of genocide, which would not have happened if it weren't for racial prejudice. (During the Black Lives Matter protests of the summer, several statues of King Leopold II were among those vandalised.)

One of the main reasons behind the Opium Wars of the 20th-century – battles the British claimed were to defend their national honour – was really about flooding China with illegal opium[6].

An interpretation of the Russo-Japanese war of the early 20th-century from the Historian Rotem Kowner is that it could've been avoided if Russia had agreed to negotiate with Japan instead of feeling superior. Nicholas II referred to the Japanese as 'Makaki' which translates to little monkeys and refused to back down from a war[7].

And this is still ongoing today.

A report by Stonewall in 2018[8] stated: 'Almost one in four LGBT people (23%) have witnessed discriminatory or negative remarks against LGBT people by healthcare staff. In the last year alone, 6% of LGBT people – including 20% of trans people – have witnessed these remarks.'

While there's still prejudice in the UK, this is much better than the situation in other countries. At the time of writing this, it remains *illegal* to be gay in more than 70 countries, with around 10 of these countries serving the death sentence.

Gender inequality is another pressing concern: in Saudi Arabia women have only been able to drive in since 2017, in Russia women are still restricted in their freedom to choose their profession, and in the UK, the gender pay gap remains significantly wide (an average disparity of 17.3%, according to official UK figures for 2019[9]). Additionally, the more recent transgender equality issues are only starting to really be discussed worldwide. Why has this taken so long?

Study of the past should be more than just a learning and regurgitating 'facts' – it's an opportunity to form your own opinion of events based on wide research and as many different accounts as possible. That's why I believe the History taught in school should provide a wider view of the world and the many societies, cultures and beliefs within it.

Controversy stems from multiple opinions, multiple versions of what is right and wrong. But these multiple opinions lead to a diversity of voices and it is only through multiple perspectives and opinions that a greater understanding can develop.

There will always be controversy over which periods of history should be taught and examined; over the messages these select historical periods convey, the mistakes that were made, battles fought and reasons for them. Those who 'lost' and those who 'won'.

This careful balance will always be hard to achieve, and yet the first steps towards it are to widen the discussion so we can recognise the problems with the current system and set about the first steps towards change. Indeed, this very chapter and book could be seen to be controversial for going against the commonly accepted beliefs of the UK educational system. And that's good! This will add to the debate and encourage future discussion.

Key Point #4: History is Politics

Big historical events tend to link directly to politics, and political decisions are often the reasons behind conflicts. As such, I was slightly flustered when big political words were thrown around the classroom as it took some time to fully understand them.

These words included those listed below, which I have provided basic definitions for:

- **Capitalism:** Wherein a country's trade and businesses are controlled by private owners for profit
- **Communism:** A country's trade and business are under common ownership
- **Totalitarianism:** A government that acts as a dictator and prevents any opposition
- **Imperialism:** Expanding a country's power and rule to other countries by force
- **Neo-colonialism:** The use of power and pressures to control another country
- **Utilitarianism:** A moral belief that promotes actions that provide the most happiness
- **Altruism:** A moral belief of acting selflessly for the happiness of other beings
- **Revisionism:** The rejection of traditional beliefs about historical events

Are you starting to see a pattern here?

Over time I came to switch off whenever I heard a long word that ended in '– ism'. Maybe you partially glossed over these words when you saw them too.

While the links between political power and historical events are mentioned in school, political concepts are generally left to Politics classes, which is an optional subject taught at A-level.

The moral concepts are left to some other class, such as PSHE, or Moral Philosophy, both of which are optional for a school to teach at any age.

When big words are mentioned it can be confusing. Especially when it detracts from the simple historical perspective of learning about dates and events.

And yet, Politics and History will always have that overlap. By using some of these long '-ism' words to illustrate periods of History, it would allow for a greater association between the subjects. Incorporating elements of Politics would allow for a more in-depth understanding behind the politically driven motivations behind certain actions.

Now, I'm not suggesting these '-ism' words, and many other Politics-related words be drilled into the minds of eager historians, as I know few students, if any, who would be excited to rote-learn them all.

What I am suggesting is that the concepts behind these big words, and their origins be better incorporated into understanding History, not only to help prepare students for the transition to learning History at A-level and beyond, but to also reinforce that at its core, History is all about people, and people will always have differing moral and political beliefs.

Recommended reading

The following books are a selection of alternative views and insights of historical events, from an overview of the entire history of humans in *Sapiens*, to Miller's fresh take on classic Greek myths and *The End* which looks at why Germany carried on fighting WWII to Chang and Halliday's revelation that Mao Zedong was responsible for more deaths than Hitler or Stalin.

> *Sapiens: A Brief History of Humankind* – Noah Yuval Harari
> *The Song of Achilles* – Madeline Miller
> *Circe* – Madeline Miller

The End – Ian Kershaw
Mao: The Unknown Story – Jung Chang and Jon Halliday

SCIENCE

Science. A word that encompasses discovery, research, advancements in many fields and new developments.

Science can be used to provide links to understanding the past (what happened to the dinosaurs), the problems of today (finding a vaccine for Covid-19) and the answers for the questions of tomorrow (how we could live on Mars).

When GCSEs were introduced in 1988, students could choose two of the sciences to study – boys commonly dropped Biology while girls tended to drop Physics.

The 'double' (or 'combined') science GCSE course was then brought about to allow students to study all three sciences in the same amount of teaching time – the double course would cover a reduced syllabus for all three sciences in the teaching time it would normally require to teach two. This would be an easier alternative to studying each of the sciences separately in the 'triple' GCSE course.

An unfortunate outcome of this arrangement is that over time this has led to a greater divide between schools in deprived areas where the triple science course is less likely to be offered, and top grammar/independent schools where triple science is the only option.

This triple science option is preferred by the government, employers and scientists as its broader subject base means it prepares students for STEM-related careers, where vacancies are often difficult to fill.

For a subject based on curiosity and questions, it is remarkable how few questions students are encouraged to ask at school as they learn a series of simplified facts. I wonder how many questions your science teachers refused to answer at school because 'the answer is too complicated at this level' or dodged by saying 'I don't know' to quickly move on.

This section will go through each science subject in turn, summarising the overarching flaws with how science is taught and why this poses a real problem for students after education.

PHYSICS

Ah, Physics.
What was the first thing that popped into your mind when you read that word?

Did you think of a convoluted equation, not understanding the subject and being glad that you dropped it? Or did it conjure the phenomena of gravity, discovering new particles and planets and all the sci-fi technology such as teleportation that we could one day achieve?

Physics is a very broad subject. It covers topics from energy changes to motion and forces; waves, electricity and magnetism to radioactivity, particles and stars. From the very small, *strange* fundamental particles that are quarks (yes, also the name of a quark!) to large yellow dwarves like our sun. Not to mention all the formula booklets with their helpful equations, such as F=ma, E=mc^2 or V=IR.

One could argue that Physics is the basis of all science.

The concept that energy cannot be created nor destroyed is fundamental to Physics. Chemical reactions require energy (E_A) to undergo, and biological organisms require energy (ATP) to live.

The very device you're reading this on required engineering skills based on a good knowledge of the subject (i.e. electrical circuits).

And yet, nearly every year fewer students choose to take Physics at GCSE and A-level, largely because it's perceived to be the 'hardest' of the all the sciences.

Key Point #1: Physics will always be hard when everyone tells you it is hard – teachers should do more to help remove students' mental barriers to the subject

Physics is not the easiest subject in the world, but I do believe part of its reputation comes from the way it is currently taught in school.

Let's start by looking at the persistent myth that Physics is 'hard'.

I've listed five reasons below:

1. Physics requires a good knowledge of Mathematics; especially at A-level certain topics in Physics require a prior understanding of a mathematical concept, i.e. exponentials and logarithms in the topic of radioactivity or differentiation and integration to derive certain formulas.
2. It requires a lot of graphs, tables, algebra and the ability to constantly alternate from specifics to general concepts.
3. Physics involves learning a lot of theories to understand how concepts and formulas were discovered. It can be confusing for students to have to understand old theories only to find out later that they're wrong.

4. The abundance of formulas and reliance on formula booklets can cause students to panic, leading them to apply formulas randomly in the hope that one will work. This, in turn, inevitably leads to an overall lack of understanding of the concepts behind the formulas.
5. Even when the laws of Physics are understood, there are still exceptions which can be frustrating to some (e.g. black holes or the recent analysis of 'strange metals', which have varying electrical resistances depending on their temperature).

If any of that sounds familiar, it's because I used to feel the same.

Personally, I thought of Physics as hard because I continuously failed to understand the subject; my confidence slowly eroding away as I answered questions with wrong answer after wrong answer, all of which served to reinforce the above beliefs.

In a bid to boost my confidence, my teachers dropped me to a lower class set. I know, it sounds counterintuitive, but it gave me the opportunity to properly understand what I was learning as I was able to learn at a slower pace than the higher set. In time, I realised I might actually be good at Physics. Before long, I was able to complete the given work faster and my peers were asking me for help.

Breaking this negative mindset about the subject is key to motivating and supporting students from the very first lesson – that way you'll not only have the opportunity to learn new concepts but also to develop the confidence in your abilities that you'll continue to do so, no matter how 'challenging' the subject becomes.

Nobody should be discouraged in studying a subject they have chosen to study at GCSE or A-Level simply because they struggled with it in the first few lessons.

In some other subjects – say Drama – students who hold themselves back because of reinforced negative beliefs and stigmas are often automatically encouraged to change their mind and to overcome their mental blocks.

Why not Physics? Because it has a reputation for being 'hard'?

If governments and employers want more students to be studying STEM subjects, such as Physics, to GCSE and beyond in order to fill the growing number of vacancies in the field, it's my belief that teachers should find ways to change your previous preconceptions about a subject and allow you to discover it for yourself by removing any limiting beliefs in your 'abilities' you may have.

Key Point #2: The current GCSE syllabus restricts the opportunity to learn through experimentation, either guided or unguided which prevents students from making and learning from their own discoveries in active learning

Physics has the potential to be a very hands-on subject. There are so many ways to see the subject in action in the classroom before learning about the theories behind what's observed. For example:

- Throwing an object across a classroom illustrates projectile motion.
- A pulley and weight can be used to show the direction and size of forces.

- Building a circuit with a series of lights, voltmeters and resistors allows electricity to be seen in action.

Yet for many syllabuses at GCSE and A-level the 'practical' aspect of the examination is taken in an exam hall, where the questions describe a theoretical practical that students are meant to have covered at some point in their studies.

And when these topics are explored in a classroom, teachers mainly describe the theory and background first before allowing students to do an experiment, causing the experiment itself to be the lesson activity to look forward to, and the theory is the 'boring' task to complete before then.

What if this process was inverted?

Let's say the lesson started with giving a pair or group two light gates, a trolley, slope, weights and a stopwatch and asking you to play around with the equipment for the first few minutes of the lesson with the teacher then slowly introducing the concept of speed = distance/time or acceleration by encouraging you to try new little experiments and record data.

This 'discovery method' was the same way that scientists originally derived many formulae; the only difference in this case would be that students would already be provided with the 'relevant' equipment for each experiment – this would allow any relevant risk assessments to take place beforehand too.

By learning as a group or pair and seeing what works and what doesn't, and comparing results and ideas, the class turns into one collective team effort in deriving a formula, allowing students to feel they've made their own discoveries themselves. The 'theory' then serves to back this up.

Wouldn't this make you more likely to remember what you are measuring in each case and what formula to apply?

Just as connections and links are being made between students, they're also being made in the neurons in the students' brains.

Indeed, there have been numerous studies that show the benefits of active learning over passive listening, including a 2019 study at Harvard that showed students felt as if they had a greater retention of knowledge when taught by active learning compared to lectures when learning Physics[1].

Learning by doing, either in the classroom or in the home could be one way to improve the way new concepts are introduced, encouraging students to have an inquisitive nature, complete further research, and ask their own questions before they are limited to a syllabus.

Homework in this case could be to design a similar experiment using different equipment at home and then record this data. Again, this encourages experimentation, personal preferences and learning methods other than simply reading a textbook.

So why is this approach not used?

Time constraints could be a factor. It is often quicker to ramble through the theory behind a topic and set practice questions as homework than allow students to investigate it for themselves and encourage discussions.

Money is certainly part of it. While some schools may have the funds to buy a scanning electron microscope, others can barely afford to replace broken equipment and only have enough equipment for five groups of six students.

Impracticality and danger also come into play. (Only the teacher is able to demonstrate a radioactivity experiment using a Geiger counter due to health and safety reasons, for example.) For quantum physics, on the other hand, doing an experiment is practically impossible – unless your classroom is inside the quantum realm!

Some students, too, may be resistant to the idea of setting up their own experiment, thanks to those preconceptions of how 'hard' it's going to be. Therefore, they are primed for failure before they even start.

Even a world-class electrical engineer charged with fixing the circuits of planes and space rockets had to have started somewhere – I believe that all students should be given the level of guidance that they need to have the confidence to try and fail, try again and fail better (to paraphrase Samuel Beckett's famous line) so that they might have the satisfaction of having their own 'eureka' moments when the concept clicks into place.

This will benefit students greatly in showing them how fun Physics can be.

During my A-level Physics lessons, my classmates and I were bewildered and surprised when our teachers instructed us to spend two weeks undergoing our own projects – it wasn't part of the syllabus and so (we thought) wouldn't play any part in helping us prepare for upcoming exams.

However, looking back, by allowing us the freedom to choose our own experiment, create our own data and carry out our own research, we became more motivated to discover more about a topic, even if it was off syllabus.

My project had a Forensics spin on it and involved looking at the different shapes of blood drops from different heights. Understandably, I couldn't use blood so used a substitute of water and red food colouring, noting this change in my brief write-up.

To understand my data, I researched basic fluid dynamics involving the Reynolds number which would not normally be covered until studying the subject at university, (even though at that stage I had no intention of studying Physics beyond A-level).

My write-up was no doubt very basic, using simplified Physics (most likely incorrectly). However, I enjoyed the process of doing the experiments and feeling a sense of accomplishment for doing some research in a field of my choosing rather than being restricted by the syllabus.

If I'm honest, I felt a little bit relieved by this freedom.

Wouldn't you?

This approach is taken in the IB (International Baccalaureate) equivalent of A-levels which encourages independent investigations and write-ups in the Sciences (and Maths) alongside an extended essay on a topic of the student's choosing. More subjects are taken for IB exams than for the more in-depth A-levels and this maintains a student's breadth of knowledge and allows them to make connections between the Sciences through personal discovery.

Sure, allowing every student to undertake their own projects at GCSE level may be hard to implement due to a lack of funding and allocation of available resources. But think of the upside – generations of students inspired by Physics rather than fearful of it.

That's not just worth striving for, but something I believe is achievable for schools to make a reality.

BIOLOGY

The study of living organisms (and viruses, depending on your viewpoint on whether a living organism needs to be able to have cells and replicate on its own to be 'alive').

Whether we like it or not, we're all slaves to our biology. We all must eat, sleep, use the toilet. Our physical features, who we're attracted to and unique metabolisms are all dictated by our biology.

Ecology, cells, plants, reproduction, cancer, energy production and evolution are a few of the topics covered in Biology at school.

In order to teach and examine these concepts, parts of topics are heavily simplified so they're easier to understand.

This is definitely a better approach to teaching science and slowly building a foundation of knowledge than by being thrown straight in the deep end. For instance, learning Glucose → ENERGY is certainly a lot simpler than learning all the reactions of glycolysis, Krebs cycle and the electron transport chain.

However, if in order to simplify these concepts, the simplifications become wrong, this 'wrong' becomes bad science.

Key Point #1: Simplifications currently taught in school can be misleading to students

Do you remember the equation for photosynthesis, the reaction by which plants convert sunlight into energy?

Water + Carbon Dioxide (+Sunlight) → Glucose + Oxygen

Simple, yes. Correct? Not quite…

When presented in the style of a chemical equation, the above implies that water and carbon dioxide mix together inside a plant using the energy from the sun and then glucose and oxygen come out of the reaction.

However, would it surprise you to know that the water and CO_2 molecules never come into contact with each other? In fact, they couldn't be further apart in terms of their respective roles in photosynthesis – the sunlight interacts with the electrons in the water to provide the energy required for the plant to undergo a process of carbon fixing where it can form glucose (and other sugars) from carbon dioxide.

So why is this simplified version taught if the method it implies (shown in the equation) is at best misleading if not, upon closer interrogation, wrong?

If the answer is to make it easier for students to be motivated to learn scientific concepts, then I, for one, would very much like to tell whoever made that decision that – as we progress through our scientific education from GCSE to A-level, and from A-level to university – it's demoralising for students like myself to be continually told that everything we were taught before was wrong and an oversimplification.

Yes, more recent scientific discoveries can disprove old theories, but that's not a suitable excuse to continue to purposefully teach inaccurate simplifications.

Or is the simplification there to discourage students from asking questions about the material and therefore make it easier to teach? If so, doesn't this undermine the inquisitiveness and communication skills that the Science curriculum purports to encourage, while also leading students into a false sense of understanding?

Perhaps the simplification is there because it's easier for examiners? When you consider that GCSE science papers are often graded using a set mark scheme, there would seem to be some truth in that. It might also explain why final marks often go up following a re-mark by a more qualified examiner.

It's one thing for students like me who go on to study science at a higher level to be disillusioned like this, but what about all those students who stop after GCSE? This leads to an additional problem: they're less likely to realise that the simplifications they learned were wrong in the first place, so carry that misinformation with them.

There are ways to simplify scientific concepts in Biology and other GCSE Sciences, without making them wrong, (or at the very least misleading,) some of which I've outlined below:

Glucose + Oxygen → Energy + Carbon Dioxide + Water
Unsurprisingly, the equation for respiration is also an incorrect oversimplification; the glucose and oxygen molecules never come into contact let alone react with each other.

Exercise requires oxygen
In fact, sprinters mainly use anaerobic respiration which doesn't require oxygen, but this builds up an 'oxygen debt' which is then

paid back in the period of rest straight after the period of physical exertion.

Going to the toilet is excretion

Excretion is the removal of metabolic waste products mainly from the lungs, kidneys and skin – such as breathing out CO_2. The removal of the undigested food and drink we ingest is technically called egestion. This makes the term excrement somewhat misleading.

Elements are made up of circular electron shells which are filled by electrons for the totals of 2,8,8

The 'shells' are comprised of subshells which builds to 2,8,18,32. The actual position of electrons can be anywhere within a subshell.

Electricity flows from the positive end to the negative end

Well, current flowing from + to − is known as conventional current only because this was mistakenly assumed to be the case when electricity was first discovered. Really, the charge carriers, the electrons, flow from the negative end to the positive end (electrons are negatively charged).

There's no gravity in space

It's still there! It's just a lot weaker.

Deoxygenated blood is blue because veins are blue

In this case the deoxygenated haemoglobin absorbs the red light and it's blue light that is reflected back to our eyes. Deoxygenated blood is dark red in colour.

We have five senses: sight, smell, hearing, taste and touch
While scientists are still unsure of the exact number of senses we have, there are certainly more than five. Proprioception, the ability to always know where your hands are even when your eyes are closed, is an example of an 'additional' sense.

All men are XY and all women are XX
Although rare, as well as triple variants such as XXY there have also been cases of men who are XX (known as XX male syndrome) and women who are XY.

All enzymes and substrates work in a lock and key method
There are a various number of methods through which substrates and enzymes can interact. One particularly humorous sounding method is the Ping-Pong Bi-Bi mechanism – it involves the first substrate binding to an enzyme and forming into its product before the second substrate binds to the enzyme.

Enzymes reduce the energy required for a reaction to occur
This is misleading and often misquoted by students (as I can attest to from my days at school). Enzymes provide an alternative route for a reaction that requires less energy on top of the original reaction route. An analogy of this is providing a tunnel through a hill. You can still walk over the hill if you have enough energy, but now there is also a tunnel if you have less energy.

Of course, concepts should be simplified to make them easier to understand (and I do acknowledge that some of my examples are more pedantically incorrect than completely wrong). However, a simplification that misleads or misinforms simply to make the 'answer' match an exam mark-scheme is the wrong approach.

Would you ever be taught a concept in Mathematics, or a date in History to be told a few years later to forget it because it was wrong?

Why is this approach used in Science?

Both the Science curriculum and examinations need to be altered to prevent these misconceptions from being learned by students who believe them to be correct because they are awarded marks for repeating them. If simplifications, such as the respiration equation, continue to be used in exams, they should be followed by a question which briefly asks why the equation is not entirely correct, so that students are able to demonstrate that they fully understand the concepts they have been taught.

These misleading simplifications could have the unintended effect of discouraging students from undertaking their own evaluative thinking or asking open-ended questions and doing further reading and research into a topic they enjoy.

Key Point #2: Students should be given a solid understanding of basic immunology as an essential component of GCSE Biology

Next up in our analysis of Biology, a case study! Yay!

Let's start with a brief look at viruses.

What is a virus, exactly? By definition, it's an obligate (restricted to one particular function) intracellular parasite that requires a host cell to survive.

In other words, a virus is a very small agent that has to inject its own DNA into the cells of living organisms (such as humans) to complete its main function – which is to reproduce itself as many times as possible.

Viruses are a special type of microorganism that can cause disease (pathogens). They can enter a human host through direct contact of infected droplets on the mouth, nose or mucosal membranes of the eye, bypass through the skin barrier because of cuts or through indirect contact when a person touches an infected surface before touching their eyes, nose or mouth.

Coronaviruses are a family of viruses, discovered in the 1960s and given their name because their infectious particles look like a crown when viewed under an electron microscope – 'corona' means crown in Latin.

Covid-19 (CoronaVirus Infectious Disease 2019) is the name given to the virus by the WHO (World Health Organisation) on the 11th February 2020. Its scientific name is SARS-CoV-2.

Yes, the virus is related to SARS (or to give its proper name SARS-CoV) which, according to the WHO, had its first reported cases in the Guangdong province of Southern China in 2002 before affecting 26 countries and resulting in more than 8,000 cases in 2003[2] (WHO, 2012).

Another member of the coronavirus family is MERS (Middle East Respiratory Syndrome) first identified in Saudi Arabia in 2012.

Coronaviruses have been around for a long time and will continue to cause colds long after the Covid-19 pandemic. Yet, many of the same people who had never heard of the term before early 2020 also believe a vaccine will act as a magic bullet that will kill the virus and end the whole 'Covid threat'.

Unfortunately, the reality of this situation is a little more complicated.

Even armed with some knowledge in Biochemistry and Virology, I've struggled to keep up with the 'science' around certain mask rules. It's hardly surprising, then, that so many members of the public clearly feel the same.

A few examples of inconsistencies that I observed include:

- Staff working in supermarkets/retail who spent long hours stocking produce in a shop didn't have to wear masks though they have an opportunity to spread the virus onto their consumer goods or directly to customers on the shop floor.
- Customers who decided to eat/drink inside cafes who spend longer than a customer who orders a quick take-away are also exempt from wearing a mask (many of these places do not enforce any kind of tracing system when it comes to eating in).
- Members of the public who incorrectly wore masks that do not cover their nose (the majority of people breathe through their nose), or who immediately removed their mask after boarding public transport thus nullifying the protective qualities a mask would provide to others.
- People who have had a positive result from a Covid-19 Antibody Test and believed that they had become immune to the virus.

I'm sure you have your own things to add to such a list.

And yet, throughout all of this, one of the main messages sent to us from the government was to use 'common sense' when making decisions during the course of the pandemic.

I would argue that with members of the population leaving secondary school without a solid understanding of basic diseases and their behaviour, advising the use of 'common sense' to prevent the spread of a virus is as useful as trying to assemble a flatpack wardrobe from a well-known Swedish retailer without realising you have the wrong instruction manual.

What were you taught with regards to that most ubiquitous of viruses, the 'common cold', for example?

Did you learn that when you reach for the paracetamol, your symptoms aren't relieved because the medicine is helping to kill off the virus but because it's suppressing certain immune responses that in turn cause that runny nose, ever-lasting cough and other symptoms? (Or that even though paracetamol has been used by the general population for a long time, there's still an open line of enquiry amongst pharmacologists about how exactly paracetamol works once metabolised?)

Or even that the 'common cold' isn't caused by one virus, but several? Around 40% of colds are caused by a rhinovirus. Others include RSV (respiratory syncytial virus), and coronaviruses.

Once viral particles have been detected by the immune system, it takes up to 72 hours for a full (adaptive) immune response to ensue, which is when you start to show tell-tale symptoms such as a runny nose, dry cough and high temperature. These aren't always caused by the virus itself, but by your own body's immune response. Coughing, for example, is one of the body's most basic defence mechanisms. Raising the temperature of the body is also another primate response that allows certain immune cells to function better. You can be contagious before you start to show any of these symptoms.

During the months of May and June I briefly volunteered in a local hospital working with some HCAs (health care assistants) and nurses. I was saddened to hear about all the HCAs, nurses and doctors who had risked their lives coming into work over the lockdown period and had suffered from Covid-19 because they had caught the virus from patients who hadn't been tested upon arrival.

Covid-19 may have a lower death rate compared to SARS and MERS but one reason why it has become a global problem is because it is more infectious with a basic reproduction rate, or R_0, of 2 – 2.5 people[3]. Surely all patients who went to hospital over the lockdown period should have been tested immediately rather than when they started to show symptoms? This could've prevented some spread of the virus from the general public to front-line workers, who were desperately needed during the lockdown period.

The Covid-19 pandemic is a great example in how it has exposed the lack of public knowledge of immunology and related issues. Obesity is a risk-factor for Covid-19-related mortality because obesity itself has been shown to increase a person's vulnerability to infection by viruses[4]. People who are obese contain higher amounts of adipose tissue (aka body fat!) which can be used as reservoirs by viruses such as HIV. Adipose tissue expresses a higher amount of the receptor ACE-2 (angiotensin-converting enzyme 2) which is a known target receptor for Covid-19 [5,6].

Of course, obesity itself can be caused by a lack of exercise, unhealthy diet, genetic factors and other pre-existing health conditions and can lead to Type II Diabetes which is already a growing health crisis for being a comorbidity regardless of a viral infection such as Covid-19.

The lesson to be learned here is that a solid understanding of basic immunology should be incorporated as an essential component of GCSE Biology.

A better understanding of ALL viruses would not only potentially help decrease the spread of infection in the case of another wave/pandemic, but everyday viruses such as the common cold.

CHEMISTRY

Walk around a school on an open day and chances are you'll see experiments such as setting bubbles on fire, creating a silver mirror in a test tube, or watching a fake volcano explode.

If you're lucky, you might even get to see a banana or flower that's being smashed with a hammer and exploding into fragments having been 'frozen' by liquid nitrogen.

TV shows show criminals cooking up narcotics and other controlled substances in *Breaking Bad* to heroes somehow synthesising any chemical antidotes required for a plot to progress (thinking of you, *Marvel's Agents of Shield*).

This fascination with pharmaceuticals, explosives and cool reactions makes Chemistry one of the most exciting subjects to learn at school – no wonder they entice students and parents with all those experiments on open days.

So how is it, that once they get you into the classroom Chemistry can seem so much less exciting than these demonstrations suggest?

Key Point #1: More real-world chemical reactions should be discussed in the classroom

Aside from needing to resort to showing the occasional YouTube video to demonstrate a particularly dangerous reaction – e.g. how dropping caesium in water causes a rapid reaction so explosive that it can shatter the container – most of the experiments undertaken as part of GCSE and A-level Chemistry can be completed using school lab equipment.

Chemistry is a subject that by its very nature can cater for not only written/book learners, but those who are visual or auditory learners too. Even the word effervescence (fizzing) is an onomatopoeia.

The boredom starts to sink in when the theory comes out. Balancing equations. Learning the definitions for an element, compound and mixture. Asking your teacher about a special element at the bottom of the periodic table only to be told that you didn't need to know about it for your exams, so it wasn't important.

That's because a key aspect of reactions is to describe the process and the colour/shape/outcome that the reactants become which is a lot more memorable when seen first-hand, even when, for safety reasons, some experiments have to be undertaken by the teacher.

Doing an experiment yourself is encouraged more in Chemistry than in the other sciences, perhaps because Chemistry teachers have a keen eye on the fire extinguisher and Chemistry labs have more safety precautions in them than other labs.

Yet even if these experiments go a long way to offset the seriousness of the theory, collectively they suffer from a fundamental flaw.

School Chemistry experiments selected for the syllabus almost always work. The hypotheses chosen to investigate in class are almost always given by the teacher. This sort of method of choosing experiments neglects to inform students that in Science, experiments don't always work.

And sometimes, experiments and trials lead to unexpected results: for instance, the drug sildenafil was initially used to try and cure angina (chest pain) before its 'side-effects' were noticed, leading it to be rebranded as Viagra.

That's not as unusual as it sounds. In fact one of the reasons why it takes so long to produce new drugs is because even when chemists have managed to find a drug they think works, they still have to be tested in human trials of increasing numbers of people to identify any side-effects and confirm the drug is fit for purpose.

These experiments that initially produce the drug often have very low yields, which is something that's touched upon in A-level Organic Chemistry. In most tests, a score of 40-50% would be seen as disappointing; in Chemistry, this is an acceptable yield. These low yields can be due to several factors including impurities, incomplete reactions or unwanted side reactions.

Of course, performing reactions that don't work in schools wouldn't be the best way to prove a theory. But the knowledge that – in real-world labs – experiments are hit-and-miss is a fundamental part of Chemistry. As it is, students are only made aware of this if they are lucky enough to have a talk from someone working in the industry.

How could students improve their industry knowledge while at school?

Perhaps through the creation of a new topic called 'Industrial Chemistry', which would examine the real applications of Chemistry and how the knowledge learned at school could relate to Chemistry outside of academia. As a student it would be fascinating to even briefly be able to use some of the chemical apparatus used in Pharmaceutical and Chemical Labs and watch the creation of a previously known drug or compound from its chemical constituents in person or through video.

What a brilliant, and easy, way to inspire the next generation of Chemists.

Key Point #2: Chemical reactions are happening within us and all around us, not just in a lab

Learning about select examples of chemical reactions, such as a catalytic converter and fractional distillation, as are currently taught in schools are useful but can limit the scope of what students believe to be Chemistry.

Some demonstrations in schools – even some university practicals – may involve the use of out-dated technology and methods which are no longer used in the scientific community (by doing an experiment by hand, for example, when scientists more commonly automate the procedure with a computer in a laboratory).

Instead, why can't there be a greater focus on the chemical reactions that are going on around us to show students how brilliantly fascinating Chemistry can be?

Asking questions such as why crisp packets pop when opened (nitrogen gas is used to preserve them and the sound is the release of the gas) or why humans don't spontaneously combust at any given moment (dioxygen, O_2, is relatively inert at the temperatures humans live at) broadens thinking and helps to begin to appreciate the expansive nature of Chemical reactions.

Chemical reactions done in vitro (lab-based) are unable to replicate in vivo (in an organism) reactions when looking at Biochemical reactions.

The human body utilises a system of hormones and signals to control when certain reactions happen in the human metabolism that allows energy to be stored in a fed state and used when required in a fasting state.

Indeed, the simple Glucose → ATP reaction can take up a whole A1 piece of paper in order to show the hundreds of reactions and side reactions that have roles in the conversion.

In this way, chemical reactions rarely occur 'in a vacuum' outside of a laboratory setting, and nature provides great examples of how chemical reactions have been adapted for many different functions.

Whenever you drink alcohol, chemical reactions break down or metabolise around 95% of the alcohol in the liver. Around 50% of East Asian people have a deficiency in an enzyme called ALDH which causes this enzyme to work much slower than in other populations. This causes a build-up of the molecule acetaldehyde and is the reason behind the so-called 'Asian Flush'.

Other animals undergo biochemical reactions, either for metabolic purposes or for special additional features unique to that animal or species – the firefly, for instance, uses the enzyme luciferase in order to be bioluminescent.

Animals can use chemical reactions for defence purposes as well, creating noxious, toxic or poisonous substances to prevent themselves from being spotted or consumed by predators. These chemical substances can be airborne (skunk), injected into another animal (scorpion) or can be used to escape (the aquatic tree bug can discharge its saliva onto the surface of water, causing a reaction that decreases the surface tension of the water, propelling the insect along).

Chemical reactions take place on dead animals too; the process of chemical decomposition relies upon bacteria for autolysis and putrefaction.

Chemical reactions are happening in space every day, although not as obviously as the 'Big Bang'. Our Sun continues to radiate heat across our galaxy due to chemical reactions occurring in its core.

In summary, whenever there's an energy imbalance, either through nature or artificially made, a chemical reaction can occur.

Real-world Chemistry shouldn't just be reserved for open days – the wonder and fascination in the vast array of interesting chemical reactions occurring all around us should be an integral part of the school syllabus.

Recommended reading

The following books are great starting points to expand your horizons within Science, from Bad Science which is a general overview of the unscientific analysis of results to books more focused on interesting areas of Biology and Physics.

Bad Science – Bed Goldacre
Power, Sex, Suicide: Mitochondria and the Meaning of Life – Nick Lane
A World Beyond Physics: The Emergence and Evolution of Life – Stuart Kauffman
Seven Brief Lessons in Physics – Carlo Rovelli

A-LEVEL

ECONOMICS

Economics, really?

I've only selected one subject for A-level – so why this seemingly random choice? The subject isn't even compulsory.

Because the 'dry' text-book economics that's currently covered at school is very different to the kind of economics I'd like to see brought into the curriculum.

Why? Because in my opinion, Economics is the basis of financial literacy.

While you might dispute whether this would fall under the category of Economics, Maths or PSHE (Personal, Social, Health and Economic education,) I believe the core concepts of financial literacy should be taught as a key part of the curriculum in schools.

For the sake of this argument, I'm sticking with Economics.

We make economic decisions every day. Students leaving university begin their life swamped in debt. The self-employed and business owners must sort out their taxes every year either with an accountant or themselves. Even if you're on a payroll and that's done via PAYE, you need to constantly balance your wages with your bills and spending with what comes in every week or month with your pay cheque.

I repeat: every single one of us will make thousands of financial decisions throughout our lives – actions that fall under 'microeconomics', which focuses on individual small businesses and consumers alongside the basic rule of 'supply and demand'.

Macroeconomics, on the other hand, refers to the wider economic model – think of all those well-known images of stock traders standing in a large room in Wall Street or the City with their big screens of green and red numbers, representing the changes in the aggregate economy.

Economics might be defined by Investopedia as: 'a social science concerned with the production, distribution and consumption of goods and service'[1], but in simple terms it's about the distribution of money and wealth.

Whether it is the pound, dollar, bitcoin, land or gold, there are always people who will want to accumulate 'wealth' in some form (and by extension the goods and services it buys).

Money may be what makes the world go around – however, unlike energy, money CAN be created or destroyed.

Key Point #1: Schools should make ALL students aware of the effects of financial decisions at a government level and how the general public can suffer the cost

Currencies are a relatively recent invention, having evolved out of the 'barter' system of exchanging goods and services.

Those pieces of paper bearing the numbers 5, 10, 20 or 50 are freely traded every day all over the world in their different set values. You use money every day, whether through using cash or spending electronically. But can you tell me where that money came from?

Let's start with a brief analysis of macroeconomics, touching on what's currently taught at school, before moving on to the more important points of microeconomics-related personal finance which – shockingly – is not covered in UK schools at all.

Below is a list of topics included in the macroeconomics section of most A-level Economics courses:

- Government Economic Policy
- Macroeconomic indicators including real GDP, the rate of inflation, unemployment and investment.
- Exports and imports
- Aggregate demand and aggregate supply (AD/AS Curves)
- AD being composed of consumption, investment, government spending, exports and imports in the formula GDP = C + I + G + (X-M)
- AS is composed of pricing levels and production costs in the short-run and technology, productivity, factor mobility, and economic incentives in the long-run.
- Inflation vs Deflation
- Debt vs Equity
- Commercial banks vs Investment Banks and the role of Central Banks in monetary policy
- Fiscal policies (taxation)
- Trade and cash flow between countries
- Currency exchange rates
- Economic growth vs development

Governments and government-sanctioned institutions are responsible for controlling the levels of inflation, taxation, imports and exports as well as the wider task of determining how the national budget is shared out.

This might sound straightforward enough, but it's anything but – as the UK vote to leave the EU in 2016 demonstrated. Achieving Brexit has meant the government has had to review many of the policies in the above sectors in order to prepare for new arrangements no longer bound by EU agreements.

Large-scale economic decisions can be short-term, too. The government's Eat Out to Help Out scheme, devised to boost consumer spending in the hospitality sector throughout August 2020 and help struggling businesses in the immediate aftermath of the Covid-19 lockdown, is one recent example, along with other temporary financial initiatives brought in at the time.

But where does all the money used to cover such schemes come from? (The Treasury estimated Eat Out to Help Out to have cost £50 million in the first third of August alone[2].)

Likewise, the furlough scheme, which covered the payroll of salaried workers by up to as much as 80% during the lockdowns, of which a tailored version – designed to help bring furloughed workers back into businesses – is still in force at the time of writing.

Or the outstanding student loan payments that, if not cleared off by students within their 30 year-terms, are expected to be paid off by the government?

Where does the money to pay for such schemes come from?

Loans are one answer; selling off government bonds another. However, these are short-term solutions (if they even really count as 'solutions' at all).

In the longer term, the government is likely to increase taxes and costs for the public, an early example of which is the TFL bailout, in which congestion charge costs have increased and, after the lockdown over Easter 2020, now operate daily in central London while free travel on TFL services for under-18s and the elderly during peak times have been temporarily suspended.

Raising taxes instead of lowering them may seem counterintuitive but lowering taxes may only provide a short-term boost to consumer spending and the growth of businesses.

Another option is for the government to continue to print more money (an act known as quantitative easing, wherein central banks create money by buying government bonds), in a bid to stimulate the economy. This can also decrease the purchasing power of the currency in question and reduces the cost required to pay back fixed government debt.

It's a risky strategy and one that, if left uncontrolled, can lead to hyperinflation – a famous example of which happened in 1920s Weimar Germany when money became worth literally less than the paper it was printed on.

Now, I'm no financial expert, but even I can see that increasing taxes and devaluing the pound will have a great impact on reducing the average person's post-tax income and the amount of goods and property they'll be able to buy.

In this way, the general public will suffer far more immediately and for longer than the rich and other elite members of society, who have the resources to weather an economic recession.

It doesn't take a financial genius to see that if taxes increase we'll be the ones who end up paying for those so-called 'discounts' we received in August 2020.

Ouch. But won't increasing taxes cause the rich to pay our more too?

Not necessarily. Because in lots of cases the 'rich' and their businesses pay only minimal taxes – and I'm referring to legal, encouraged alternatives rather than the morally ambiguous (some might argue, downright dishonourable) methods of using off-shore tax havens or shell companies.

Even if the rich were all taxed in a proper fashion, and companies didn't leave the UK if taxes on them were raised, this would only pay off a few billion of the government's increasing debt, which was £1.98 trillion in July 2020 (that's £1,980,000,000,000).

While this would be a good start, it would only solve a small part of the problem.

Another example of how the general public is hit the worst is the increasing amount of job cuts and redundancies for workers in the aftermath of the Covid-19 crisis, while those on the boards of the very same companies continue to receive their bonuses even days before a company is declared bankrupt.

Why? One reason could be that the ignorance over general economic issues leads many people to 'trust' an economic set-up that doesn't necessarily have their best interests at heart. Another could be the many poor long-term financial decisions that people make with their money throughout their lives due to a lack of financial literacy.

Regardless of whether they choose to study Economics, students should be made aware of the basic points raised above on government debt and policies to enable them to make more informed decisions about how they spend their money, not to mention the decisions being made for them by the government.

Key Point #2: Students should be aware that the 'security' of saving money in a bank is not as financially 'future-proof' as it used to be

Now for the real-life parts of Economics – your finances.

The most basic financial advice you've probably been given is to always have less money going out than you have coming in, with most people confident the right thing to do with any excess is to save it in a bank. But that isn't always wise.

Say you have indeed saved money by working hard over the past few years and deposited it in a bank.

The bank balance you see on screen at an ATM isn't the money in your account but rather an electrical 'IOU' note from the bank to you, which acts as a money substitute that you can spend whenever you use your debit card.

In other words, not actual money.

So where does the real money go?

A bank loans out part of the money it receives from deposits and other sources to make more money for itself. Which is all well and good as long as the economy's stable, but if it isn't?

In the case of a crisis such as Covid-19, if everyone scrambled to the bank to take out their hard-earned savings it would result in what's known as a 'run' on the bank and the bank would panic. They wouldn't be able to produce all the money as cash and would place a daily cap on the amount of money that could be withdrawn each day by each customer.

Now you probably knew that already, but did you know that the banks are also able to create money through debts?

This concept isn't hidden. In fact, it's openly discussed on the Bank of England website[3] which states: 'If you borrow £100 from the bank, and it credits your account with the amount, 'new money' has been created. It didn't exist until it was credited to your account… Banks create around 80% of money in the economy as electronic deposits in this way.'

In other words, physical currencies are only a very small proportion of the 'actual money' in the UK. The general public still drives this money by taking out loans from banks and allowing the bank to 'create new money'.

While the limits on how much money a bank can create are regulated, they are, ultimately, businesses that are looking out to make a profit.

OK, you say, fair enough – that's part of Economics. And if they're regulated, then the customer is always being looked out for, right?

Not always. I'm sure you're heard of PPI (payment protection insurance), which was a form of insurance offered on loans that were mis-sold by a variety of banks and other financial institutions to over 45 million consumers (many of whom had it applied without their knowledge), leading to the pay-out of billions of pounds in compensation and resulting in significant damage to the UK lending industry.

But back to savings – and the so-called 'best practice' of depositing yours in a bank.

Since the economic crisis in 2008, interest rates have continued to fall, with returns from savings now so low (around ~0.1%) there is little value to be keeping your savings in a standard bank savings account.

As a result, many people have turned to the stock market or have invested in ISAs instead. Opening a Cash ISA from the age of 16 or Stocks & Shares ISA from the age of 18 allows you to save up to £20,000 free of income tax (protected by the FSCS compensation scheme in the UK, which guarantees up to £85,000 worth of savings, depending on the type of account).

The stock market is notoriously volatile, so many people turn to independent financial advisors and/or invest in managed funds that allow someone with expertise to oversee their investments (usually for a fee).

But that is no guarantee that an investment will be successful. (Land and gold, on the other hand, are physical commodities of which there's a limited amount and as such their value cannot be as easily manipulated – which is one of the reasons why gold, particularly, not only holds its value, but tends to go up in value when economic times are tougher.)

What about a pension then? In the UK employers are committed to make a minimum contribution to compulsory pension schemes. Which is 'free money', right?

Yes and no.

Rather than this money being given to you directly as part of your salary for you to invest as you choose, it goes into a saving plan that you have no control over, could decrease in value at any time (most pensions are pegged to the stocks and shares), and that you have to pay taxes and fees the moment you wish to access. (Though, it should be noted, employees can opt out of company pension schemes if they so choose.)

Money is a more ephemeral concept than many people believe – remember that when it comes to making plans for your so-called financial securities.

Key Point #3: A good education is no guarantee of a job for life

Job security is a thing of the past.

Few students leaving university will stay in the same company, let alone the same job until they retire.

The job market is continuously changing and has already changed so much over the past couple of decades in terms of contracts, working hours and pension plans.

Zero-hour contracts are even worse, as employees don't know when they'll be needed and are therefore likely to earn variable amounts each week making financial planning even more difficult.

Why is there so little preparation in the current school system for these huge changes in the market?

Students, especially those about to leave academia, need to have an idea of how to plan for their economic future and how to 'future-proof' themselves. They should be able to think outside the old lines of thought which may have worked for the previous generations but may no longer be as dependable in the current day.

Getting a job is not the only option you have, and yet so many students believe that they have to study in order to get a good job and a pay cheque that's representative of their academic efforts.

Why is so little still being done to teach students about alternative life options other than the route to a more 'traditional' career?

At schools and universities, career workshops, careers fairs and career programs are heavily encouraged. The paths to internships, apprenticeships, and alternative ways to learn new skills and pursue your own personal development, far less so. Entrepreneurship programs, how to analyse investments, how to earn your own money through your own assets, passive income streams or basic personal finances aren't covered in as much detail, if at all.

These are all things I believe should be covered in far more detail in school. But above all else, remember that the only person responsible for your long-term financial security is you.

Key Point #4: Don't forget about your taxes! How much you pay could be entirely down to how much you know about the tax system.

What do you think when you read the word TAX?

Your contribution towards the economy?

Funding government spending and various public expenditures?

Tax evasion schemes and how the rich should pay more?

Or in the most depressing outlook, death and taxes being the only certainties in life?

Everyone who earns over their personal allowance of £12,500 must pay tax on the excess, whether they're self-employed, on a payroll or a business owner.

The PAYE scheme is how most people pay their income tax. If you earned more than £1,000 through being self-employed or £2,500 from other untaxed income including rental properties, investments or foreign income, then this must be declared via a self-assessment form.

National Insurance payments are deducted as well when a tax assessment is completed, using your personal NI number.

This is a smoother process when you're employed or once you're registered with HMRC, but this process is still rather confusing for students.

Student taxes can seem to be more complicated to calculate than adults', as students can have a collection of employed and self-employed roles during the holidays and not in term-time.

If you're student who works part-time do you have to pay taxes? If you earn through self-employed work – private tuition or babysitting, for example – do you need to declare this?

If it's cash in hand, is it advisable not to declare the transaction, as many adults seem to do?

Perhaps most importantly, when do (self-employed) students have to complete their first tax form so that they're not fined?

Let's break it down.

The tax year runs from 6th April – 5th April of the following year.

According to the GOV.UK website[4], you have to pay:

- Income Tax if you earn more than £1,042 a month on average – this is your Personal Allowance (this works out at around the £12,500 per year figure)
- National Insurance if you earn more than £183 a week

The simplest case is if you're a student who's employed. Then your employer will deduct your taxes and NI if applicable before paying your wages through the PAYE scheme. When you leave, the employer will provide you with a form called a P45, which you can then give to your next employer to ensure that you're placed within the correct tax band.

The National Insurance payment required is 12% of your gross salary if you earn less than £4,167 per month, or 2% if above. This rate can change in certain situations, such as whether you're married or have more than one job[5].

As the tax brackets depend on an average monthly income, sometimes you could be overcharged on your tax payments, however HMRC is (according to itself) normally very efficient in returning any excess tax that you have paid. Alternatively, the P50 form can be used to claim back overpaid tax.

The tax-free personal allowance applies to everybody regardless of what they earn. The current income tax bands in England, Northern Ireland and Wales (at the time of writing in August 2020), is shown below:

Tax Band Name	Taxes Paid for Each Bracket	Tax Rate (%)
Personal Allowance	< £12,500	0

Basic Rate	£12,501 to £50,000	20
Higher Rate	£50,001 to £150,000	40
Additional Rate	> £150,000	45

You may have noticed that the second column has the name, 'Taxes Paid for Each Bracket'. This is because you can pay several different tax percentages on the same salary.

Suppose you had a high-earning job that paid you £69,000 per year. You'd pay no tax on the first £12,500 earned, 20% on the next £38,500 (taking you up to £50,000) and then 40% on the remaining £19,000.

Overall, you would pay £7700 + £7600 = £15,300 in tax, so would have £43,700 left over.

Your NI payment would be deducted at a 2% rate from the gross earning of £69,000.

This leaves £42,320 as your salary.

If you're self-employed, then calculating your taxes becomes your responsibility. To fill out a Self-Assessment requires bank statements and receipts in order to complete it correctly. Once you're registered as either self-employed and earning untaxed income over £1,000 (which does indeed include payment for tutoring and babysitting!) or a partner in a business, you'll be given a Unique Taxpayer Reference (UTR).

The deadline to complete your tax return is the January after the end of the tax year if submitting the form online (so 31st January 2021 for the 2019/2020 tax year) or the end of October if submitting a paper form. (It's worth noting it takes time to initially register, which could bring the deadlines closer by about two weeks.)

If you're a volunteer and claim back out-of-pocket expenses, or receive a grant or a bursary, these can be collected tax-free.

Were you ever told about this at school or university?

This explains why accountants are normally the first port of call for those who have no idea how to complete their tax return or want to pay someone to complete it for them.

Yes, it could be argued that as this is a task often covered by your employer or outsourced to an accountant it's not something everyone needs to know, but as paying taxes is a compulsory annual task set by the government shouldn't some of this at least be introduced and understood within a government-run school curriculum?

If students were shown the basics of how to pay tax and in what situations they would be expected to declare their earnings, wouldn't this save future hassle for HMRC in the long run in chasing up unpaid taxes?

Perhaps you knew someone at university who rented a property and forgot to fill out the form to declare them exempt from their Council Tax payment? Did they even know they could claim this?

The concept of taxes, what taxes you need to pay after school, and how to register on HMRC could be easily introduced into GCSE Maths or even in the 'Economics' section of PSHE as a compulsory small course (one single class for 6 – 8 weeks perhaps?) for all students.

Key Point #5: Student loans are more of a tax than a debt

We've covered taxes, so let's look at debt.

Yes, it fills me with dread too. We're not alone.

Millions of Britons are in debt. According to the Office of National Statistics, the 'total household debt in Great Britain was

£1.28 trillion in April 2016 to March 2018, of which £119 billion (9%) was financial debt and £1.16 trillion (91%) was property debt (mortgages and equity release)[6].

Which is a lot.

An overwhelming majority of students who go to university leave with a mountain of debt alongside their sought-after degree.

But is this really debt?

(NB: I use the terms debt and loan a lot in this section, so let me quickly clarify their definitions. A loan is something you can apply to take out from a bank or from another person, and in doing so you will accrue a debt that is required to be paid back. While all loans are debts, not all debts are loans – other examples of debts include bonds or mortgages. The words debt and loan are interchangeable in most circumstances. The collective debts and loans comprise part of the total liabilities of a company.)

As it stands, if you started your university course in England and Wales after 2012 and earn over £26,575 a year (Plan 2 Loan as stated on the GOV.UK website[7]), under the current scheme, 9% of your wages are automatically paid to the Student Loans Company. (This threshold is subject to change each year in April). If your income is under the threshold, you don't have to currently pay back any of the loan.

Interest is added from the loan immediately from when the first payment is given to you which is 5.4% when you are studying and then depends on your income once you leave university.

While parents or some high-earning students occasionally want to pay off the loan early, unless the loan can be cleared in one lump-sum (in which case, the question could be raised of why you needed the loan in the first place!), there's very little benefit in doing so if, in time, the loan clears itself.

The debt is written off either 30 years after the April of your first repayment or if the event it happens first (sorry!) you die.

Now, I've mentioned student loans in the 'debt' section because the name suggests it to be one.

However, I would argue that in many ways this 'loan' is more of a tax.

Let me explain.

Firstly, the amount you repay is determined by SLC based upon your earnings as declared to HMRC and are deducted from your salary automatically. Secondly, most students won't end up paying off their loans in 30 years. Finally, unlike 'real' debt, these repayments – even if you fail to clear the full amount – have no bearing on your credit score.

All of which explains why a growing number of individuals and groups are campaigning for student loans to be relabelled as a tax in a bid to remove the confusion surrounding them – of whom MoneySavingExpert founder Martin Lewis is one of the most notable[8].

So as you see, debt isn't as straightforward as simply earning money – even when it's simply about owing money.

Key Point #6: Debt can be good and bad; it's knowing the difference that matters

Did you know that debt can be both good and bad?

Yes, really! That's why it is worthy of its very own key point.

An example of good debt is paying a deposit for a property and taking out a mortgage which is then paid off by renting the property or part of the property to a tenant. The debt can then be cleared using the tenant's repayments, leaving you with a valuable asset that you can go on to sell or leverage against future investments.

Similarly, taking out a few loans on a credit card that you're careful to pay back before any interest is due will help boost your credit score – which, in turn, will help when it comes to taking out any bigger loans in future (e.g. for that mortgage).

Even business take out loans as part of a calculated risk that whatever they're using the funding for will build on the investment provided by the loan and turn it into profit.

'Bad' debts on the other hand are – unsurprisingly – things such as buying items on credit when you are unable to afford it, especially when using a high-interest credit card.

With so many adults stuck in the never-ending pit of debt, why isn't a basic Debt 101 syllabus introduced in schools to try and prevent the adults of tomorrow from falling into its downward spiral?

You might argue that people will always want new things that are out of their so-called price-zone – the latest fashion item, games console or car.

However, I believe a poor financial education is partly to blame. (Just look at those lottery winners who receive more money that they know what to do with and still end up bankrupt after a few years.)

The government is under no pressure to introduce a basic financial education. On the contrary, it actively encourages us all to get out there and spend – a message that's been accelerated post-lockdowns – while the government itself is struggling with its own trillions in debt.

On a wider scale, the world practically runs on debt, and without it, this could bring the world closer to an inevitable financial collapse, with Covid-19 accelerating this process.

Even setting aside what they might lose through defaults, debt repayments provide banks with healthy profits. However, alongside the spending and borrowing that fuels it – by individuals, businesses and entire countries – the delicate balance that keeps the financial world, as we've designed it, spinning can at any time threaten to collapse. Just as it's looked to do at various times before and – as the ripple effects of Covid-19 are spreading ever further out – is threatening to do again, even as I type.

Perhaps it isn't money that makes the world go around, but debt.

Key Point #7: A knowledge of human psychology would provide students with a better understanding of why financial transactions take place in the 'real world'

Economics is about money, assets and all the rest, but what else?

What fuels the markets? Whether to buy or sell, how to best make a profit (or fail to) – even the basic concept of supply and demand – all fundamentally comes down to the same thing.

Human decision-making.

And the choices people make – both collectively and individually – depends on their psychology. Think about it: people and businesses are 'hopeful' they'll make a profit or 'fear' making a loss. Emotion is at the heart of every decision we make.

And for businesses, psychology is increasingly a driver in that decision-making.

Supermarkets put the most expensive products at eye-level as this grabs your attention better. Until the practice was banned, they would put sweets near the tills so customers would be tempted to impulse buy when queuing. They alter the tempo or volume of their store music to make you shop faster or slower. The very design and colour palette of a shop interior can subliminally influence your response to it.

And that's not all.

Numbers are presented in ways that make promotional deals seem even bigger – 25% off for an item that now costs £3 rather than £4 as the number in the percentage is bigger than £1 off. On the flipside, £8,000 sounds more impressive than a 25% decrease in the cost of a £32,000 car.

Something similar plays out in the stock market.

If investors and traders are feeling confident the market rises, like a Jenga tower, in what's known as a 'bull market'; too much worry and just like that Jenga construction the market is likely to tumble quickly and dramatically as those same investors and traders sell (turning the 'bull market' into a 'bear').

Understanding human psychology, therefore, is an important part of Economics.

So why, in my Economics textbook at school, was there barely one chapter on the psychology behind the market, let alone the wider economy?

When the know-how is there, the right words can be used to persuade someone to fix something or change almost anything, including their behaviour towards a difficult task. When completed correctly, this can work on anyone (yes, even that difficult uncle).

Think of a children's TV program. What's the first one that comes to mind?

Are you thinking of *Bob the Builder*?

It's not that astonishing if you were.

I've used the psychological trick of priming to try and persuade you to think of precisely that show by deploying words such as 'know-how', 'fix something', 'difficult task', 'completed correctly', 'yes [we can]' and even the word uncle (to subliminally link to the phrase 'Bob's your uncle') in rapid succession in the previous paragraph. As well as the referencing to 'constructing' a Jenga pile a little earlier before.

And this was me being incredibly heavy-handed. Think what a real expert might be able to persuade you to do.

The point is that psychology is hugely influential and can take many forms, from the obvious to the subliminal. It's also one of the reasons why stocks, bonds and mutual funds, which all fluctuate according to the mood of the market, are so unstable.

And why gold, which is a limited 'real' resource, tends to become more valuable the more volatile the market is. It's dependable whereas 'assets' that are really nothing more than numbers on a balance sheet or encrypted into a long line of code are not.

Company stocks and currencies, on the other hand, can plummet drastically after one bad comment or action by someone in a position of power.

If, for example, news that a certain company was exploiting underpaid labour in the UK leaked, investors might worry about the effects of an incoming political storm and may well sell off stocks based on that fear.

Human nature is inevitable, and emotions rule us all.

Which is why, I believe, it should be essential to investigate Psychology more deeply as part of the Economics syllabus at school.

Recommended reading

The following books are a great introduction to improving your financial literacy and to understand more about how money is made in the world around us from the stock market to governments.

*Rich Dad Poor Dad (*and others in the *Rich Dad* series*)* – Robert Kiyosaki

Tax Free Wealth – Tom Wheelwright

The Man Who Solved the Market – Gregory Zuckerman
Start Up Nation: The Story of Israel's Economic Miracle – Dan Senor

SO WHAT IS THE POINT OF SCHOOL?
(and how you can improve your future)

If this book was a videogame, this chapter would be the boss.

Which funnily enough could be exactly who you'll end up reporting to if you become an employee. Which, when you come down to it, might be the very thing school is *really* for.

After all, school has already primed you with many of the qualities that are looked for in an ideal employee:

- You must turn up at set a time (and will be reprimanded if you're late).
- You have to request permission in advance if you want or need to be absent. Or call in sick if, at short notice, you cannot come in.

- You're committed to being there for a specific number of hours over set days and with a set lunch break.
- You're rewarded for putting effort into your work and are told off for slacking and misbehaviour (or even kicked out).
- You need to learn vast swathes of information that are useful for a selective purpose and which you look forward to immediately forgetting and never needing again.
- You're required to only develop the skills you need to succeed within the framework of that environment and most probably will be actively discouraged from taking any risks.

Society as we've created it needs employees for the current economic model to function.

One criterion the majority of employers use when recruiting for a position is the grades a student receives at school or university.

And many parents and students believe good grades are required for a successful future – as shown by the outcry over the use of a flawed algorithm to award students with their GCSE and A-Level grades in August 2020, which highlighted how rigidly students (and those around them) are fixed to the belief that their entire worth is based on their examination results.

They believe if they have an AAB/ABB instead of an AAA, and miss their first choice university place, their future is directly under threat. And yes, it's devastating at the time, but what they haven't been taught to understand is that their grades don't define them or the many options in front of them that can help them achieve what they desire in their lives.

While it doesn't seem this way when you're in the school system, having more grades and certifications by your name doesn't guarantee a better job or the ability to set up a strong financial future for yourself and your future family.

Top independent schools and elite universities often churn out highly ranked students with plenty of profitable skills and ideas, who are pre-selected in the admissions process – students who then go on to make up a considerable proportion of the workforce across financial, consulting or management firms, and who are highly sought after by employers.

Employers who will then likely make these new employees undergo specific training so they become able to complete a specific function in the way the company wants – learning 'company policy' and 'company values' along the way.

And what of those who take their education to an even higher level?

Even someone who qualifies as a doctor or professor might still struggle to find a job.

Just because they're super-knowledgeable in one specific area means next-to-nothing if they are forced to look elsewhere to make a living.

Take the Humanities for example. Its subjects provide students with a wide knowledge base, an ability to understand the world from different viewpoints and transferable skills in research and creativity.

But very few people with a History degree end up as Historians. Indeed, a report from February 2019, published by Prospects, a Careers Advice website, stated that 53.4% of History graduates were employed six months after graduating – with 27.7% going into further study – and of those employed, 18.7% ended up in retail, catering and bar work[1].

Yes, that's just a snapshot of a period shortly after graduation, but how many of them expected to find themselves without the 'good job' they had been primed to expect throughout all those years of school and higher education?

And all that's before we even get started on how quickly even long-established career paths can be disrupted by technology and other changes.

School is a wonderful concept. It gives children a structured education, encourages social skills and provides a level of structure to early life. But it could also better foster an environment of continuous learning and more actively encourage the development of inter-personal skills and creative exploration that, in my experience, and those of my peers, is so sorely lacking at this time.

Regardless of our grades, we all have the potential to network, learn from others and even create our own million-pound ideas.

Yet, without the knowledge of how to turn those ideas into action, and how to make that dream a reality, those ideas are worthless. Students should be given the tools they need regardless of the path they choose in life.

As it stands, I'd argue that the current curriculum and current format of examinations prepares students for a very narrow path of studying a set number of subjects and the belief that some kind of university degree is needed to become more employable, instead of considering other options, such as apprenticeships.

Firstly, while it's true that many employers look at educational qualifications as a way of weeding out applicants long before they decide who they are going to interview, a growing number of them place much greater value on the 'soft skills', motivation and charisma, that applicants might bring to a role.

Employers value transferable skills, including teamwork, communication and problem solving. And yet teamwork is somewhat limited in schools where most scholastic tasks are expected to be undertaken independently. Where teamwork is easily achieved, it tends to be in extra-curricular activities, such as team sports, drama productions or mini projects that are 'valued' less than the conventional academic subjects when it comes to awarding grades.

Transferable skills, such as how to communicate effectively (and the power of persuasion) or active listening and empathy, are rarely picked up solely from following the school curriculum.

Nor is the concept of maintaining good mental health.

Our mental health is incredibly important throughout our lives and only very slowly is that understanding being introduced into schools (due in part, perhaps, because of the persistent stigma surrounding the discussion of mental health problems). However, according to a recent Samaritans report, suicide was still the leading cause of death for those aged 15–24 in 2018, with 759 of these young people taking their own life[2] – the very ages that are supposed to be the 'happiest and simplest times of our lives'.

Three quarters of these deaths were males, with the highest rates for young men aged 20 – 24[3]. The report stated academic pressures and bullying were common reasons for suicides in young people aged under 20[4].

In 2019, the largest mental health survey ever conducted on UK university students (a total of 37,654) by Rethink Mental Illness revealed one in ten (9.4%) think about self-harming often or all the time, and that almost half (44.7%) use alcohol or recreational drugs to cope with problems in their life[5].

And let's not forget the discrimination many students will face for everything from sexuality, race, gender, ability and upbringing. In one 2017 Stonewall study[6] alone, one in eight LGBT people aged 18-24 (13%) said they had attempted to take their own life.

Meanwhile, students of a more entrepreneurial mindset can struggle in school. Individuals who tend to hate following set instructions without being able to ask why. Who don't understand why students have to compete against each other in an exam, fight for grades instead of working together, or why so much emphasis is placed on remembering useless material over a short period of time simply to obtain a piece of paper. And who, when they want to do something differently or take risks, are advised against it under the current system.

Such students may not achieve the highest grades because of the way subjects are approached and examined. This doesn't mean they're stupid. Rather, they possess a different kind of intelligence – one that's arguably suited to real life over the very narrow educational environment that UK schooling has become.

Bill Gates and Richard Branson are just two examples of well-known entrepreneurs who dropped out of academia only to became more successful than their peers once they entered the 'real' world.

Am I saying drop out of school?

Not exactly.

But I am suggesting you might want to reconsider your mindset and current beliefs about the school system.

If you're going to school and university to get a job, then you probably are best to stay doing exactly what you're doing in school, and yes, in time, you'll most likely become one of those employees that, as I've outlined, businesses require to function.

If, however, you're beginning to question what you're actually learning about in school and university, and how this is vastly different from the skills you want to be developing, then ask yourself the following questions:

- Do any of your teachers seem bored to be teaching you straight from the textbook?
- Do any of your teachers have a problem with the way the current curriculum is taught and how it's preparing you for life after school – and if so, why?
- Do any of your teachers actually have any real-world experience in the subjects they teach, other than a degree and a teaching qualification, and are they willing to share any of the mistakes and experiences they've had?

If your answer is yes to any of the above, lucky you – you've found a teacher who is willing to teach above and beyond the narrow constraints of the curriculum. I recommend you speak to them and find out more as soon as you can - this could be your first step to a new way of learning!

If, on the other hand, the answers are all no, don't despair. This is an opportunity to network to find some like-minded individuals.

Then you might find some real answers.

The answers you seek are out there: it's all about asking the right questions to the right people.

So, who's that?

Well, that depends on what you learn from them and how you choose to use that information.

I've looked to entrepreneurs throughout this book as the key examples of the kind of future aspiration and success that's not commonly encouraged at school.

That's because successful entrepreneurs are admired by many people for being able to achieve something that they personally feel that they would never be able to achieve. Entrepreneurs strive to apply their knowledge to have a 'real-world' impact by finding a solution to a real-world problem.

They don't have the limiting belief that they require a 'classic education' to reach their goals and this explains why they are not so upset on results day when they don't get the grades they think they deserve.

Of course, there are other paths that may be more 'right' for you. And discovering that is an exciting part of your journey.

Perhaps your 'path' is to make a difference in the world through an act of social or political change – whether that's tackling a worldwide problem such as global warming or addressing the continuing racial/gender-based injustices that so many people continue to face every day.

It could be that your passion is the pursuit of a very singular personal achievement – you might even aspire to go as far as becoming the world's best at whatever that may be. If that's what you want, don't let anyone hold you back – this is your time to shine!

It's possible that your aspiration is humbler – you may simply aspire to meet your dream partner and be able to support your family in their needs and live 'happily ever after'. (And by humble I don't mean easy; one goal is just as valid as another and 'happy ever after' isn't simple by any means – the important point is that it's the one that is right for you).

Dreams like these may seem vague and far-reaching, but they share one thing in common: they're achieved by setting goals not by reading textbooks.

Goals that have a defined endpoint such as:

- Being able to retire at the age of 50
- To make a certain amount of money in a month
- Learning a new skill in a holiday
- To reach a target weight in three months
- To be a parent by the age of 40

Goals can be fun too and may even seem a little unrealistic at first:

- Visiting every continent
- Experiencing zero-gravity
- Be in a TV show or movie (as an audience member, extra or star!)
- Enjoying a scuba diving experience
- Writing a book (That's one off my bucket list)

In other words, your goals can be whatever YOU want. As many self-help books note, writing down these goals in a place you can see them every day will help to drive you towards them and find ways to make them a reality.

Once you begin to question the limitations of school and understand there are other paths you can follow, you can truly begin to examine your options.

Instead of going after jobs because you 'need' the money, go after your passions. Learn and improve upon existing ones you find interesting and let your growing reputation speak for itself. You may even create a new job that allows you to do what you love and find you can support yourself from doing so. In a world where Korean ASMR YouTubers are paid to eat food on camera and 'influencers' are paid to take selfies, even what might, at first, seem to be your silliest ideas may have some merit.

If you do take a 'traditional' job, think of it as any training ground for you to learn from. Don't be afraid to move on to something else once you've learned all you can from a role – a successful life requires progression.

If you can't quit your job because you need your pay-check to survive, look at building your skills in your spare time and explore all the other activities you could be doing.

Perhaps you could set up a small side-business which one day could make you more than your job so you can quit.

Or you might want study a subject you always wanted to, but were told you couldn't at school, expanding your horizons and developing your curiosity on the way (the internet is full of online courses, both free and paid-for). You could even find ways to use your new knowledge to your benefit further down the line.

If you want to be able to use new skills in the real world, consider applying for internships, volunteering opportunities and jobs that you find interesting and can learn from.

Even if you are one of the lucky few who's in a job you love, don't allow yourself to be become complacent – these days there is no such thing as a 'job for life'.

Your job is no longer a guarantee of long-term financial security.

Your job is not the sole activity you should be utilising your skills for – your pay-check should not be the only reason you get out of bed in the morning.

Yes, we live in challenging economic times, but to quote Albert Einstein: 'In the midst of every crisis, lies great opportunity.'

Did you know that in the Chinese language, the word 'crisis' is formed from two brush strokes, one representing danger and the other opportunity? Or that the root definition of the word in English is derived from the Greek word 'krisis', which means a time where an important decision must be made for better or for worse?

In other words: seize the opportunity.

To be prepared to do so, I recommend that you:

- Never stop learning (the things you want to learn). Remember: it's not about the exam grade, but the simple satisfaction of being able to accomplish or perform something new that you enjoy.
- Don't give up, and don't let mistakes upset you.
- Forget the teacher who has a go at you for getting a low grade and instead remember that you cannot improve without making mistakes.
- Stay open to them and new experiences and opportunities will come to you. Never lose sight of building your own skillset and working with those who raise you up rather than tear you down.

School is a great learning experience but it can narrow the mindsets of many bright students and reinforce the idea that they must follow a set path throughout life.

Students have so many great ideas, thoughts, abilities and passions which make them such unique individuals. Yet, when they become adults, they all seem to converge towards the same work ethic, actions and day-to-day activities.

At the risk of sounding like the mentor who picks up the movie hero after they have catastrophically fallen on their face, my advice would be:

Your passion, skills and drive are the roots that allow your tree to grow. Your school education helps you grow and blossom and then guides you into growing into a tree of set proportions. Your tree has the potential to be any size and shape you want it to be. What tree do you want to nurture?

We all grow up eventually, but how and where is completely down to you.

Having read this book, your journey is just beginning.

Get out there and grow.

Recommended reading

The following books cover a wide variety of topics that I believe are greatly helpful in life – from networking, knowing how the words you use can have a powerful impact, having a strong mindset to a basic idea of how a start-up works.

The Definitive Book of Body Language – Allan & Barbara Pease
How to Win Friends and Influence People – Dale Carnegie
Methods of Persuasion – Nick Kolenda
Limitless – Jim Kwik
The Lean Start-Up – Eric Ries

The following book is a great mirror of this one and covers the US educational system – with more detailed factual analysis:

The Case against Education: Why the Education System Is a Waste of Time and Money – Bryan Caplan

MY REALISATIONS

I mentioned who I am in the About the Author section at the beginning of this book.

Now I'd like to tell you my story.

As I wrote then, I've had a series of realisations over the past few years that have made me rethink my life choices, question the current educational system and eventually lead to my decision to write this book.

As promised, I'd like to share them with you here.

Realisation 1: All schools care about are your grades

I have a confession to make. When I was younger, I made a HUGE mistake.

I thought a good education was going to set me up for life; that if I wanted a better paid job, then I needed to work harder at school. To get a better chance at applying for a top company, I thought I needed the best grades.

So I tried my best to work hard. I read around my subject. Did many of the after school and lunchtime activities I was encouraged to do in a bid to improve my knowledge. Sat in the front of the class to become more engaged in lessons. Wanted to score the highest in tests. Was called a 'teacher's pet' by my peers. Was bullied. Turned to books instead of going outside.

It didn't help that my parents encouraged me to follow this lifestyle. They only wanted the best for me and honestly believed that the way to set me up for that was a good education – just as their parents had before them.

And where did this lead me? It was one of a handful of factors that led me down a rabbit hole.

Into depression.

I was suspended from my secondary school for reasons surrounding my poor mental health a few months before sitting my A-level exams in Biology, Chemistry, Maths and Physics. It goes without saying that my parents tried continuously to overturn the decision, as they wanted me to be able to go back.

This was one of the most difficult times for me. I could play the 'blame game' and blame the school for the level of bullying and discrimination I was receiving from pupils and teachers that had led to my depression – which affected my academic and personal life – and caused the school to kick me out so I could 'get better'. Or blame myself for thinking that alcohol could 'fix' my problems because I was too ashamed to talk about them. But none of that would do any good. And now, looking back, I'm actually grateful I had this experience.

Why?

Because it was in those dark times that I realised exactly who my true friends and support network were, and I was forced to focus on my mental health rather than revise for my upcoming A-levels.

I had to confront the situation I was in, the mistakes I'd made along the way, and figure out my next steps.

I set myself a goal to get into Oxford – to reach my predicted grade of A* A A – and so, every day, in between going to meetings with counsellors and spending time with family, I worked by myself from home with occasional help from my friends to achieve my goal. Even though I was struggling, with the support from those genuinely concerned about me – both emotionally and in preparing for my exams – I was able to focus on three of my A-Levels: Biology, Chemistry and Maths.

I still spent whole nights crying and had my ups and downs, but in the back of my mind I knew I wanted to get into Oxford. It was my salvation, my ticket out. Close to the time of my exams, after a long series of discussions back and forth, the school let me return to complete my examinations – and as you know from the intro to the book, I managed to match my predicted offer (and get a C in Physics).

My school sent me an email congratulating me on my achievement and added me to their growing list of Oxbridge leavers so that I could become another statistic to bolster to their all-important rankings.

This applies to all schools, whether independent or state. Individual teachers may want their students to do the best they can, but the heads of schools want the best results to bolster the school's rankings and performance.

But this was not their achievement, it was mine.

When it came to the leaver's ceremony, I refused to shake the headmaster's hand.

Looking back, the whole period was a life lesson unintentionally taught by my school that has stayed with me forever. Ironically, I learned more from this experience that I did from reading textbooks in class.

Many parents select schools based on its academic performance. Especially if the school is independent and charges a fee. These schools have entrance exams, so they select pupils who they believe will obtain high results, increase the school's performance or maintain their reputation and inspire the next round of eager parents to send in their applications for their children. And so the cycle goes on…

This was the first time I lost faith in the school system.

You might have had a similar experience – not the same as mine, necessarily, but one in which you felt as if all the odds were stacked against you, and yet you continued to try. The injustice that you faced could have been more challenging and upsetting than mine.

However, I am sure that you came out of it stronger. And if you're still going through it, I want you to know that there's hope.

Realisation 2: Many people are stuck in boring jobs

In the summer before starting university, I worked full-time in a department store in London. It was my first experience of wearing a suit, coming into work, having a rota, a pay-check, colleagues, as well as being introduced to office politics, gossip, and being scolded for lateness. I brought my youthful energy to the role I was going to perform, working in the Customer Services department.

I remember my first day properly on the job (not counting the induction days when I was told how great the company was until I was red in the face). I had been kindly introduced to a fellow colleague, who was going to introduce me to the system that I would be using to help customers and carry out my role.

The system was a simple one: you pushed the call button on screen, the next customer ticket number from a list came up – first on your screen then on the big board in the waiting area outside, alerting the customer with that ticket to come to your desk. You helped the customer with their query, completed and signed a few forms, then called a new number. And so on.

Maybe it was because I was curious. Or naïve. Or because, thanks to that youthful energy I mentioned, I was reckless.

I asked my colleague a simple question:

'Can you change which ticket you call?'

I remember my colleague staring at me blankly before responding, 'I don't know. I haven't tried before.'

I moved the mouse cursor over the list of tickets on screen and clicked on the ticket that was second in the list. Then I clicked call, and both my colleague and I were surprised to find that ticket was called. I'm sure the customer with the first ticket must've been confused, sitting in the waiting area wondering why their ticket had been missed out.

This little experiment changed me. It made me realise how many employees simply blindly follow protocol, day in, day out, without ever wondering what might happens if they were just a little bit curious.

I appreciate some people might fear losing their job for exploring out of their bounds. And that there may be a sense of comfort in following a usual, familiar pattern for others.

However, I quickly realised that while I enjoyed some aspects of work, I didn't enjoy following the same procedure again and again. The customers were pleasantly different and each one had their own unique story and query to complete. Before long, however, their experiences quickly blurred into one.

I tried asking customers to guess my age to liven up the conversation. In my formal black suit, sitting behind a computer, passing signed documents across a big wooden desk, most customers guessed I was around 23 or 24 years old. When I mentioned that I was just 18, some customers reeled in horror and quickly re-examined the documents I was handing them as if they now thought I must be incompetent and had made mistakes on the form. Others looked astonished or questioned whether I'd dropped out of the school system and was doing some sort of apprenticeship.

As boredom sank in, I did play around with the system some more. I was intrigued by what else I could do. I can only hope it's been updated since, as any staff member could very easily put a spanner in the works in the entire waiting system by calling random customers to random staff desks.

You may be asking me, 'Why didn't you tell your manager about the flaw?'

Well, for one reason, I was worried that I would be told off for not following the rules. Be told that I shouldn't be playing around with the system, and perhaps even be subject to 'disciplinary action' for doing so.

Secondly, I didn't feel confident. I was there for a brief summer job before my university journey began and didn't feel I was in any position to mention to a superior that the system that they were dependent upon was flawed.

I was soon shown tips and tricks by fellow colleagues to make it look like they were working when they weren't, a few of whom opened up to me about their experiences at work.

What surprised me was the number of staff members who said they disliked their job and/or certain colleagues. The staff who felt they weren't appreciated. The staff who were desperate to switch shifts because they wanted a specific day off to be with their friends. The part-time bank staff – often students – who were begging for extra shifts in order to get more money. The staff who wanted to quit but needed a pay-check to live.

Realisation 3: Experience and passion in self-learning is worth more than any exam result

I believe that passion and being ready to make mistakes in real-world practice are more important than any exam result on a piece of paper. While a grade shows how you performed in an isolated test, it has little to no bearing on the knowledge you use, the upcoming decisions you make or your future potential.

This realisation first dawned on me during my university application process and it's been reinforced many times since.

Every student has to consider their reasons for applying for a particular university and course as their focus shifts from a broad coverage of subjects at GCSE to a narrower field at university.

As a teenager I loved Forensics. I was one of those classic *CSI* fanatics who would watch every episode and get angry when my friends pointed out how unrealistic the whole show was (yes, I know that the high-resolution CCTV footage was quite unrealistic), but I didn't care. I enjoyed the thrill of the stories and the evidence used to find the culprit(s).

I enjoyed reading the science behind the show. My teachers may have thought it was strange when I brought a book called *Poisons and Poisonings – Death by Stealth*[1] into school, but that's what I was interested in.

I applied for several (Bio)Chemistry courses in the belief that it was a subject that would allow me to build a strong foundation into the scientific basis and methods behind many forensic techniques. This would, at the same time, honour my parents' wish for me to 'get a good degree in a solid science subject'.

Though my school advised me against it based on my GCSE results, I applied to Oxford as one of my five university choices.

I was pleasantly surprised when I was then called for a series of interviews and ended up having three on one day.

Prior to the final one, I was given a series of questions to complete. When I was invited in, I went through them with the two tutors who were interviewing me, before they moved on to the topic of my personal statement – which outlined my interest in forensic science.

My eyes lit up.

I remember asking my mother on the phone after the interview why she thought they'd questioned me about Forensics. She replied: 'To see if you are passionate to learn about Biochemistry.'

She was right. The tutors had seen my great passion for the subject and assumed I'd apply it to my studies.

In this case, I don't know to what extent my academic results and performance up until that point had been a factor. Perhaps my AS grades had got my foot in the door. But I would also argue that it was having a strong passion for a relevant aspect of my chosen subject that helped me stand out from amongst other candidates. Which was something that my school had not prepared me for.

Once they had been informed that I was going to be interviewed, I was given the opportunity to take part in several revision sessions at school and a mock interview, and had been given countless book recommendations to read. Not a single teacher recommended I brush up on my Forensics knowledge or raised the possibility that a subject I was passionate about might play some part in the process at all.

I later came to realise there's a similar process of selection at work with employers.

Thousands of jobs are advertised every year, many attracting well upwards of a hundred applicants or more for a single role.

It's often taken as a given that applicants will have some sort of degree (not having one could be the first point of rejection for many job applicants), but whittling applications by academic rankings can only go so far to trimming the crop.

In such a competitive field, true passion for a company or sector can help you to stand out – whether that's doing your research to prove your understanding of that company's motivations and goals or learning through volunteering and/or internship experiences in the same field.

And it's not just job applications.

To achieve anything in life requires passion.

Academic accomplishments may be a great starting point, but passion is the extra not-so-secret ingredient that will get you there.

Chances are you'll have experienced the difference between learning a subject because you had to (a struggle), compared to something you have a genuine interest in.

Your passion will shine through no matter where you go and what you strive to accomplish. And the important point to note is that it doesn't have to be academic.

That entrance interview was the first time I realised I didn't have to be restricted by learning the curriculum enforced upon me to strive for a goal.

Yes, you might have to hit certain academic 'marks' to get you in position. However, the real examination is life – and it's one in which you have to form your own questions before you know what answers you want to seek out.

In my case, this led me to look for guidance and answers in places I'd never considered turning to before.

Not academic textbooks.

Books of real personal experiences written by people who were willing to share their struggles, journey and life lessons.

People like Robert Kiyosaki, Allan & Barbara Pease, Dale Carnegie and Jim Kwik.

I began to recognise a key theme in many of the books I was reading. That in order to learn how to do something, I had to actually do it – and be ready to make mistakes.

I learned more about the UK healthcare system and the true reality of how the NHS was coping in the midst of the first Covid-19 lockdown by volunteering 'on the front line' for two months than I could ever get by reading a book or the internet.

I saw first-hand the outcome of the mistakes that the healthcare service and government had made in the period leading up to the pandemic before it was heavily criticised in the media. I heard real accounts from those on the front line about how they had struggled during this time and the lessons they'd learned too.

But you don't have to go through such a dramatic experience to begin to understand it's the 'doing' that's important. Consider the following examples of real-life problems that have required real-life mistakes to improve:

- When you first learned how to iron your clothes or correctly use a washing machine, did you read a book about it or ask someone to show you? How many times did you accidentally ruin some of your clothes?
- When you wanted to play a piece of music, did you sit a theory exam or practise on your instrument? How many wrong notes did you play before you could play the piece correctly?
- When you prepared for your driving test did you think you would pass from watching a series of how-to videos or by physically driving with an instructor? How many times did your instructor correct you?

So, don't be afraid to stray from the academic textbooks, form your own questions and make mistakes as you begin to figure out the answers.

Realisation 4: Employees are easier to replace than assets

During the summer before my second year at university I decided to take a part-time job.

I wanted to be able to have a personal trainer in the gym to help motivate me, have money to buy drinks on a night out and to occasionally buy shopping for my family at home. In order to do these, I had to find a way to earn some money.

There's a local supermarket near me where I decided to apply. As a regular shopper, I knew some of the staff already and it was a five-minute walk from where I lived.

I talked to one of the managers (I'll call him Tom) and he helped me apply via a 'Family & Friends' scheme. As with most jobs in retail these days, after completing a short online (scenario) exercise, I was invited to an assessment centre where we were given a group exercise and were individually pulled out for our personal interviews. Cue the standard competency-based questions that seems to be used by every employer in the world.

Before I could work on the shop floor, I spent almost a whole day completing a series of online training videos and quizzes on health and safety, manual handling, stock rotation, asking for ID, customer service...

Yes, I was bored out of my mind too. It seemed strange that for a supermarket that desperately needed more staff on the shop floor, they were making me spend hours in the basement answering questions on the correct temperature to store milk.

I later found out that it was all for legal reasons.

Even after all the training, I was eager to go upstairs and integrate with the team.

So, what was the first task I was given? Working the till.

When I asked one of my managers why I was always on the till, I was told, 'All new staff start on the till until they have the skills to help out more in the store.' As it turned out, all new staff were put on the till until they were no longer the newest member of staff.

Either way, I found that strange. Surely it would be beneficial for the company to utilise the strengths of their employees in order to boost productivity? And yet here I was standing behind a till because I didn't have the requisite skills to stock a shelf.

You think I'm kidding?

I assure you, I'm not.

When I did eventually 'level up' from being a till assistant and moved to stocking shelves with other staff – starting with the fresh food and then the other longer-life products – or 'facing-up' stock (in which items are simply brought to the front of the shelf to give the impression the shelves are full), I realised even these activities had their pitfalls.

While I appreciate that keeping shelves as fully stocked as possible is a key component of any retail venture, managers would assess my work as if I were a naughty school child who had handed in an essay that I'd completed in crayon – I would often be asked to 'face-up' sections again if they weren't deemed to be up to standard.

The majority of managers would get stuck in and help out, setting a good example and boosting morale to the fellow staff members, although some would spend their shift hiding in the office, watching football (yes, seriously) and only very occasionally rearing their head to critique.

Does any of this sound familiar to you?

I asked my managers and fellow staff members to show me how to complete new tasks such as scanning products that were out of stock, cleaning the coffee machines, or bringing pre-ordered parcels to customers.

Either I was told that it was outside my work capabilities as a 'new' staff member or I was shown how to perform it to then be expected to do it every shift.

The fact that there was this clear path of instructions and rules to follow reminded me so much of the school system. Being expected to complete the same tasks day in, day out, which were then examined by a manager. Having to follow a rota of set hours. Being assessed for my progress at one-on-one monthly meetings. Just when I thought my school days were behind me!

After around five months and even though I only worked two days a week, I had begun to loathe coming into work – doing the same tasks over and over again: stocking the same shelves of milk, facing up the annoying tins of beans that kept falling over or trying and failing to wrap up excess newspapers into neat piles with some string.

Finally, after one run-in too many with Tom too far, I quit.

I still go into the store occasionally and while I recognise some familiar faces, most of the staff have turned over.

Some of this will be because they have moved on to other opportunities, but if my experience was typical, I also believe such a high staff turnover is because too many staff are treated as if they're expendable and aren't valued while they're there.

How can you expect loyalty and commitment from a team if they don't feel they're valued?

Think about one of the golden phrases in retail: The customer is always right.

Is it used because the customer is always right?

No.

It's because it's easier for the company to get a new staff member than it is to get a new loyal customer.

There will always be people applying for jobs, whether its students looking for a part-time job to earn some extra money or adults who need the money to survive – and that's the case more than ever today.

How many companies, even big successful brands, have shut down stores and made hundreds of employees redundant due to the fallout from the Covid-19 pandemic?

Why have some companies tried to renegotiate contracts with their staff and threaten to 'fire and rehire' them?

Why is cutting back on employee numbers often the first solution companies turn to in order to reduce business expenses?

While those in the higher up positions in a company continue to receive their bonuses, those lower down on the shop/stock floor are being handed their notices and asked to leave. It is easier to fire a member of staff, especially during a period of economic recession, than it is to restructure a company's assets, organisation or board structure. And why should they? Ultimately, minimising debts and maximising profits are the most important goals for a business, more so than making sure each individual employee earns a pay-check.

This might explain the petty bureaucracy and power plays between members of staff but it shouldn't be a reason for it to exist.

That said, my very brief exposure to the world of work showed me how some jobs mirror a school system in which your performance is more important than making you feel valued. I'm thankful for these experiences and realisations that they have led to so far.

Including the wonderful journey I've had in writing and self-publishing this book.

So, what are my next steps? I don't know.

What I do know is that I am ready to leave an outdated school system behind me and forge my own path. One that challenges me and pushes me to the very best I can be.

What about you?

APPENDIX - NUTRITION GUIDE

A simple approach to nutrition breaks down all foodstuffs into three main categories: Carbohydrates, Protein and Fats.

Carbohydrates come from foods including bread, rice, oats and potatoes and provide a source of glucose which can be stored by the body as glycogen when not required.

Protein is found in meat, as well as non-meat alternatives, such as tofu, lentils and chickpeas, and is used to repair muscles after exercise. The building blocks of protein, amino acids, are used to form enzymes and hormones such as insulin and melatonin.

Fats are made up of triacylglycerols that are carried in the bloodstream in the form of molecules known as lipoproteins. Fat is stored by our bodies to be used as an energy source when fuel reserves are low.

Fats are also the macronutrients that most frequently come under fire for being the 'unhealthiest'.

Like most things in life, it's not as simple as that.

At its broadest interpretation, fats can be saturated (bad) as in greasy food, chips, butter or cheese, or unsaturated (good) as found in avocados, nuts and vegetable oils.

(There is also a 'third' man-made fat, commonly known as trans fats. These have been chemically altered to be more stable and provide products including biscuits, frozen pizzas and margarine with a longer shelf life. They have been repeatedly linked as a possible cause of heart disease and certain cancers.)

The principle of good and bad fats is commonly misunderstood by those who have been told to reduce their fat consumption to lose weight, who opt for 'fat-free' products instead. This avoidance of fat and reduction of fat in certain products is believed to have led to an increased consumption of refined carbohydrates that contain high levels of sugar. Fat-free yoghurts or food alternatives often contain high levels of sugar (or salt) instead of fat and as such are problematic in their own right with regard to long-term healthy eating.

A calorie is the amount of energy that it takes to increase the temperature of one gram of water by 1°C (~4.2 J). Each macronutrient contains a different number of calories, with proteins and carbohydrates having four calories per gram, fibre having two cal/g and fats having nine cal/g.

Cholesterol is another molecule that is badly understood for its dual purposes in being a molecule for good and bad. In their acceptance speech for The Nobel Prize in 1985, Michael Brown And Joseph Goldstein said: 'Cholesterol is a Janus-faced molecule. The very property that makes it useful in cell membranes, namely its absolute insolubility in water, also makes it lethal'[1].

In layman's terms, cholesterol itself is not an inherently dangerous molecule and has many beneficial uses as well as its infamous damaging role in causing heart attacks.

Cholesterol can be absorbed from the diet or synthesised in various tissues and is excreted through the digestive system or is broken down in the body. Its levels are very tightly regulated by the body.

There are two types of circulating cholesterol, LDL (low density lipoproteins) and HDL (high density lipoproteins). Lipoproteins are essentially the 'vehicles' that allow cholesterol to travel in the blood.

HDL is known as the 'good cholesterol' which can protect you from cardiovascular diseases. This accounts for a minority of the circulating cholesterol. A diet high in fibre and maintaining regular aerobic exercise can increase HDL levels.

This leaves most of the circulating cholesterol as LDL, which carries cholesterol to your arteries and increases the risk of plaque formation if allowed to accumulate. This can decrease blood flow to the heart muscle – known as coronary heart disease.

LDL cholesterol build-up can be a side-effect of a high saturated fat diet with limited exercise.

If you have a specific goal in mind, such as to lose/gain weight, then the simple calculations to find your BMR (Basal Metabolic Rate) and TDEE (Total Daily Energy Expenditure) are essential alongside any sporting activities to get results.

The BMR equation (also known as the Mifflin – St Jeor formula) is below:

MALE BMR: $(10 \times \text{weight in kg}) + (6.25 \times \text{height in cm}) - (5 \times \text{age in years}) + 5$

FEMALE BMR: $(10 \times \text{weight in kg}) + (6.25 \times \text{height in cm}) - (5 \times \text{age in years}) - 161$

TDEE = BMR * multiplier between 1 to 2 which depends on how often exercise is taken

Exercise Taken	BMR Multiplier
Rarely	1.2
1 – 3 times a week	1.375
4 – 6 times a week	1.55
Every day	1.725

Simply put, if you consume the same number of calories as your TDEE you will maintain your current weight. Eating below the TDEE will cause you to lose weight and eating above the TDEE will cause a gain in weight. Of course, the proportion of the macronutrients consumed is important, for example most athletes looking to gain muscle aim to consume 2.2g of protein per kg of their body weight.

Enjoyed the nutrition guide?
Sign up to my mailing list to learn about other life-skills NOT taught at school at *reformukschoolsnow.co.uk*

NOTES

Introduction
1. FT Online, 'Millennials poorer than previous generations, data show' published February 23rd 2018

Fundamentals – Maths
1. As shown in the book *'Principia Mathematica'* written by the philosophers Alfred North Whitehead and Bertrand Russell in the 1910s
2. Maths Syllabus, GOV.UK Website
3. Guardian Online, 'Female students outnumber males in A-level science entries' published 15th August 2019
4. FT Online, 'Women and maths — what's not adding up?' published May 15th 2019
5. A paraphrased title of an interesting maths book by Jeremy Wyndham – see recommended reading
6. OCR Website – Reformed Functional Skills: Withdrawal
7. Google Search performed on 22nd July 2020, used first search result to WorldData.Info website
8. As reported by the Education Policy Institute in August 2018
9. Called the 'hemline theory' by economist George Taylor

10. As analysed by David Ottewell on the New Statesman UK Online on 8th April 2020

Fundamentals – English
1. National Literary Trust Online – contains some rather eye-opening figures to the actual level of illiteracy in the UK
2. OECD (2016), Programme for International Student Assessment (PISA)
3. See report mentioned in 1
4. Classic Holmes Quote, useful when removing bias from critically thinking, from A Scandal in Bohemia, 1892
5. Letters of Charles Dickens Vol.3, Oxford University Press
6. Frank W. Elwell, Reclaiming Malthus, 2 November 2001
7. Department for Education Report 2013, GOV.UK Website
8. GCSE students allowed to drop poetry in 2021 exams, BBC News Website
9. Evening Standard Online, 25th May 2014 – many other online newspapers reported similar stories on the same date
10. Stonewall, July 2019 – these changes come around in Sep 2020 for England, 2021 for Scotland and 2022 for Wales.

Sport
1. Physical Activity, Fitness, and Physical Education: Effects on Academic Performance (Kohl III & Cook, 2013)
2. Can exercise improve self esteem in children and young people? A systematic review of randomised controlled trials (E, F& Hagen K, 2005)
3. Physical activity interventions for people with mental illness: a systematic review and meta-analysis (Simon, Anne, Catherine, Jackie, & Ward, 2014)

4. Obesity - NHS website

Humanities - Geography
1. BBC Future Website – Will Covid-19 have a lasting impact on the environment?
2. Excel Data from Average Roadside Gas Emissions recorded by King's College London on data.london.gov.uk

Humanities - History
1. Taken from GOV.UK National Curriculum for History
2. Life in Nazi Germany 1933-1939, BBC Bitesize Website
3. Runnymede Trust, 'How the Poles saved England'
4. Elliot, J.H, La Europa divided
5. Manuel del Campo, review of The English Armada: the greatest naval disaster in English history
6. Lin Zexu, Letter to Queen Victoria (1839)
7. Kowner 1998, Nicholas II and the Japanese Body, The Psychohistory Review Vol.26 No.3
8. LGBT Britain Health page on Stonewall website
9. Gender pay gap in the UK: 2019, according to Office of National Statistics

Sciences
1. Peter Reuell, Lessons in Learning on Harvard Gazette Online
2. SARS page on WHO website
3. Ewen et al., 2020, Nature, Coronavirus Pandemic in 5 Powerful Charts
4. Misumi et al., 2019, Cell Reports 27, 514–524, April 9th, 2019
5. Malavazos et al., 2020, Obesity Journal, Vol 28, No.7, 1178-1179, July 2020

6. Ryan et al., 2020, Obesity Journal, Vol 28, No. 7, 1191 – 1194, July 2020

Economics
1. Definition from Economics: Overview, Types, and Economic Indicators page on Investopedia
2. Eat out to help out: More than 10.5m meals claimed in first week, BBC News
3. How is money created on Bank of England Website
4. GOV.UK website – Student Jobs: Paying Tax
5. GOV.UK website – National Insurance
6. Office for National Statistics website – some very interesting data and graphs on the site about the UK population
7. GOV.UK website – Student Loans
8. MSE Online, Student Loans Mythbusting – worth a read for anyone with Student Debt

What's the Point of School
1. What can I do with my degree/history from Prospects.ac.uk
2. Suicide Statistics Report 2019 – Samaritans
3. See report mentioned in 2
4. See report mentioned in 2
5. Rethink Mental Illness, Largest Survey of university Students page
6. See Note 8 from History Section

My Realisations
1. Hargreaves, Tony (2017), well worth a read for anyone interested in forensic science and crime

Appendix
1. Joseph L. Goldstein Nobel Lecture. The Nobel Foundation

REFERENCES

Bachmann, C. L., & Gooch, B. (2018, November 7th). *LGBT in Britain - Health*. Retrieved July 18, 2020, from Stonewall: https://www.stonewall.org.uk/lgbt-britain-health

BBC. (2020, July 17th). *Life in Nazi Germany, 1933-1939*. Retrieved from BBC Bitesize: https://www.bbc.co.uk/bitesize/guides/z2932p3/revision/2

BBC News. (2020, August 4th). *Coronavirus: GCSE students allowed to drop poetry in 2021 exams*. Retrieved 8th August, 2020, from BBC News: https://www.bbc.co.uk/news/education-53645824

BBC News. (2020, August 10th). *Eat out to help out: More than 10.5m meals claimed in first week*. Retrieved August 24th, 2020, from BBC News: https://www.bbc.co.uk/news/business-53731002#:~:text=Under%20the%20scheme%2C%20which%20is,is%20capped%20at%20%C2%A310.

Campo, M. d. (2019, March). *Review of The English Armada: the greatest naval disaster in English history*. doi:10.14296/RiH/2014/2312

Chappelow, J. (2019, June 29th). *Economics: Overview, Types, and Economic Indicators*. Retrieved August 5th, 2020, from Investopedia: https://www.investopedia.com/terms/e/economics.asp

Charles, D., House, M., Storey, G., Brown, M., & Tillotson, K. (1974). The Letters of Charles Dickens. In C. Dickens, M. House, G. Storey, M. Brown, & K. Tillotson (Eds.), *The British Academy/The Pilgrim Edition of the Letters of Charles Dickens, Vol. 3: 1842–1843* (Vol. 3). Oxford University Press. doi:10.1093/actrade/9780198124740.book.1

De Peyer, R. (2014, May 25th). *Of Mice And Men and To Kill A Mockingbird among casualties in Michael Gove's syllabus shakeup.* Retrieved July 31st, 2020, from Evening Standard: https://www.standard.co.uk/news/education/of-mice-and-men-and-to-kill-a-mockingbird-among-casualties-in-michael-goves-syllabus-shakeup-9432662.html

Department for Education. (2013). *English literature GCSE subject content and assessment objectives.* GOV.UK, Department for Education. Retrieved July 31st, 2020, from https://assets.publishing.service.gov.uk/government/uploads/system/uploads/attachment_data/file/254498/GCSE_English_literature.pdf

Doyle, S. A. (1892). A Scandal in Bohemia. In S. A. Doyle, *The Adventures of Sherlock Holmes.* George Newnes (The Strand Magazine).

E, E., F, H., & Hagen K, a. C. (2005, Nov). Can exercise improve self esteem in children and young people? A systematic review of randomised controlled trials. *British Journal of Sports Medicine,* 792–798. doi:10.1136/bjsm.2004.017707

Education, D. f. (2020, July 6th). *National curriculum in England: mathematics programmes of study.* Retrieved July 20th, 2020, from GOV.UK: https://www.gov.uk/government/publications/national-curriculum-in-england-mathematics-programmes-of-study/national-curriculum-in-england-mathematics-programmes-of-study

Elliott, J. H. (n.d.). La Europa dividida (1559 - 1598). Editorial Critica, 2002.

Elwell, F. W. (2001). *Reclaiming Malthus.* Retrieved July 31st, 2020, from http://www.faculty.rsu.edu/~felwell/Theorists/Malthus/Index.htm

England, B. o. (2020). *How is money created?* Retrieved August 5th, 2020, from Bank of England: https://www.bankofengland.co.uk/knowledgebank/how-is-money-created

Ewen, C., Cyranoski, D., Mallapaty, S., Stoye, E., & Tollefson, J. (2020, March 26th). The coronavirus pandemic in five powerful charts. *Nature, 579,* 482 - 483. Retrieved July 26th, 2020, from https://media.nature.com/original/magazine-assets/d41586-020-00758-2/d41586-020-00758-2.pdf

Foundation, T. N. (1985, December 9th). *A RECEPTOR-MEDIATED PATHWAY FOR CHOLESTEROL HOMEOSTASIS.* Joseph L. Goldstein Nobel Lecture, University of Texas Health Science,

Department of Molecular Genetics. Retrieved August 4th, 2020, from https://www.nobelprize.org/uploads/2018/06/brown-goldstein-lecture-1.pdf

GOV.UK. (2020). *National Insurance*. Retrieved August 7th, 2020, from GOV.UK: https://www.gov.uk/national-insurance/how-much-you-pay

GOV.UK. (2020). *Repaying your student loan*. Retrieved August 6th, 2020, from GOV.UK: https://www.gov.uk/repaying-your-student-loan/print

GOV.UK. (2020). *Student jobs: paying tax*. Retrieved August 7th, 2020, from GOV.UK: https://www.gov.uk/student-jobs-paying-tax

Hargreaves, T. (2017). *Poisons and Poisonings: Death by Stealth*. RSC Publishing.

Henriques, M. (2020, March 27th). *Will Covid-19 have a lasting impact on the environment?* Retrieved August 9th, 2020, from BBC Future: https://www.bbc.com/future/article/20200326-covid-19-the-impact-of-coronavirus-on-the-environment

Jeffrey, M. (2016). *Results from PISA 2015*. OECD. Retrieved August 1st, 2020, from https://www.oecd.org/pisa/PISA-2015-United-Kingdom.pdf

Johnson, M. (2014, April 28th). *How the Poles saved England - another forgotten story*. Retrieved July 2020, 2020, from Runnymede Trust: https://www.runnymedetrust.org/blog/how-the-poles-saved-england-another-forgotten-story

Kidd, C. (2019, December 5th). *Household debt in Great Britain: April 2016 to March 2018*. Retrieved August 6th, 2020, from Office for National Statistics: https://www.ons.gov.uk/peoplepopulationandcommunity/personalandhouseholdfinances/incomeandwealth/bulletins/householddebtingreatbritain/april2016tomarch2018

Kohl III, H. W., & Cook, H. D. (2013). *Educating the Student Body: Taking Physical Activity and Physical Education to School.* Institute of Medicine, Committee on Physical Activity and Physical Education in the School Environment; Food and Nutrition Board. Washington DC: National Academies Press (US). Retrieved September 1st, 2020, from https://www.ncbi.nlm.nih.gov/books/NBK201501/

Kowner, R. (Spring 1998). Nicholas II and the Japanese Body: Images and Decision-Making on the Eve of the Russo-Japanese War. *The Psychohistory Review, 26*(3), pp. 211-253. Retrieved September 4th, 2020, from http://asia.haifa.ac.il/staff/kovner/kowner1998.pdf

Lewis, M. (2020, June 16th). *Student Loans Mythbusting*. Retrieved August 6th, 2020, from MoneySavingExpert:

https://www.moneysavingexpert.com/students/student-loans-tuition-fees-changes/

London, K. C. (2019). *London Average Air Quality Levels*. London AIr Quality, London. Retrieved August 9th, 2020, from London Datastore: https://data.london.gov.uk/dataset/london-average-air-quality-levels

National curriculum in England: history programmes of study. (2013, September 11th). Retrieved July 28th, 2020, from GOV.UK: https://www.gov.uk/government/publications/national-curriculum-in-england-history-programmes-of-study/national-curriculum-in-england-history-programmes-of-study

NHS. (2019, May 16th). *NHS - Obesity*. Retrieved August 2020, 2020, from Overview: https://www.nhs.uk/conditions/obesity/

O'Connor, S. (2018, February 23rd). *Millennials poorer than previous generations, data show*. Retrieved August 29th, 2020, from Financial Times: https://www.ft.com/content/81343d9e-187b-11e8-9e9c-25c814761640

OCR. (2020, February 19th). *Reformed Functional Skills: Withdrawal*. Retrieved August 9th, 2020, from OCR: https://www.ocr.org.uk/administration/support-and-tools/siu/functional-skills-575482/

Office for National Statistics. (2019, October 29th). *Gender pay gap in the UK: 2019*. Retrieved September 4th, 2020, from Office for National Statistics: https://www.ons.gov.uk/employmentandlabourmarket/peopleinwork/earningsandworkinghours/bulletins/genderpaygapintheuk/2019#:~:text=The%20gender%20pay%20gap%20among,2019%2C%20and%20continues%20to%20decline.

Organisation, W. H. (2012, April 26th). *SARS (Severe Acute Respiratory Syndrome)*. Retrieved July 25th, 2020, from World Health Organisation.

Ottewell, D. (2020, April 8th). *Why UK Covid-19 deaths are being undercounted – and by how much*. Retrieved July 21st, 2020, from NewStatesman: https://www.newstatesman.com/science-tech/coronavirus/2020/04/why-uk-covid-19-deaths-are-being-undercounted-and-how-much

Prospects.ac.uk. (2019, February). Retrieved July 18th, 2020, from what-can-i-do-with-my-degree/history: https://www.prospects.ac.uk/careers-advice/what-can-i-do-with-my-degree/history

Rethink Mental Illness. (2019, March 5th). *Largest survey of its kind reveals extent of university students' struggles with thoughts of self-harm, loneliness and anxiety*.

Retrieved August 2020, 2020, from Rethink Mental Illness.: https://www.rethink.org/news-and-stories/news/2019/mar/largest-survey-of-its-kind-reveals-extent-of-university-students-struggles-with-thoughts-of-self-harm-loneliness-and-anxiety/

Reuell, P. (2019, September 4th). *Lessons in learning*. Retrieved August 23rd, 2020, from The Harvard Gazette: https://news.harvard.edu/gazette/story/2019/09/study-shows-that-students-learn-more-when-taking-part-in-classrooms-that-employ-active-learning-strategies/

Richard, A., Weale, S., & Niamh, M. (2019, August 15th). *Female students outnumber males in A-level science entries*. Retrieved July 22nd, 2020, from The Guardian: https://www.theguardian.com/education/2019/aug/15/female-students-outnumber-males-in-a-level-science-entries

Ryan, P. M., & Caplice, N. M. (2020, May 31st). Is Adipose Tissue a Reservoir for Viral Spread, Immune Activation, and Cytokine Amplification in Coronavirus Disease 2019? *Obesity, 28*, 1191 - 1194. doi:10.1002/oby.22843

Samaritans. (2019). *Suicide Statistics Report*. Retrieved August 8th, 2020, from http://www.nspa.org.uk/wp-content/uploads/2019/09/SamaritansSuicideStatsReport_2019_AcMhRyF-3.pdf

Seagull, B. (2019, May 15). *Women and maths — what's not adding up?Financial Times*. Retrieved July 22, 2020, from Financial Times: https://www.ft.com/numberchallenge

Sibieta, L. (August 2018). *The teacher labour market in England*. Education Policy Institute.

Simon, R., Anne, T., Catherine, S., Jackie, C., & Ward, P. B. (2014, September). Physical activity interventions for people with mental illness: a systematic review and meta-analysis. *The Journal of Clinical Psychiatry*, 964-974. doi:10.4088/JCP.13r08765

Stonewall. (2019, July 15th). *LGBT-inclusive education: everything you need to know*. Retrieved July 31st, 2020, from Stonewall: https://www.stonewall.org.uk/lgbt-inclusive-education-everything-you-need-know

Trust, N. L. (2017). *National Literary Trust*. Retrieved August 1st, 2020, from What is Literacy: https://literacytrust.org.uk/information/what-is-literacy/

WorldData.Info. (2020, July 22). Retrieved from Average sizes of men and women: https://www.worlddata.info/average-bodyheight.php#:~:text=In%20the%20US%2C%20the%20average,a%20height%20of%201.66%20m.

Wyndham, J. (1998). *Why do Buses Come in Threes?* Portico.

Zexu, L. (1839). *Letter to the queen of England, from the high Imperial Commissioner Lin, and his colleagues.* The Canton Press. Retrieved September 4th, 2020, from http://media.bloomsbury.com/rep/files/Primary%20Source%2013.0%20-%20Lin.pdf

The author bears no responsibility for the continued integrity of the sources referenced.

ACKNOWLEDGEMENTS

I am hugely grateful to the following people, without whom this book in its current form would not have been possible:

My mother and older half-brother's mother for their support both throughout my writing journey and towards my mental health and motivation.

My older half-brother for his realism and telling me to 'keep it slow' that inadvertently provided me a great challenge to beat!

My editor, Catherine Jarvie for keeping me enthusiastic during the editing process and for all her efforts in cutting out the waffle and taking my initial scattered beams of thought and focusing them into a single laser.

Cat Dove for proofreading the book.

The friends listed below who provided me with their insights, feedback and encouraging messages, especially when I felt as though I had no idea what I was doing attempting to write, edit and create a completed book in four months!

Toby Noskwith, Leo Warburton, Lucas Stolle, Ashley Wong, Caroline Carter, Emma Dinnage, Charles King-Tenison, Peter Wallich, Sebastian Hatt, Julie Summers and Jennifer Greenbury.

I would like to thank Sensei Neville Tetteh who continues to boost my confidence, who lifted me up through martial arts when I was at my lowest points and never limited what I could learn. Plus, Charlie McKee, Marco Polonelli, and Reis Stainislaus, who have all strived to keep me physically fit and healthy in the gym when I haven't been sat on a chair typing (I needed the break from the workouts!).

Thank you as well to all the other people I've had conversations with who've shared their ideas on the ways in which they think the current UK curriculum should be reformed and whose stories and insights have been so useful in helping me understand different experiences of the school curriculum.

Printed in Poland
by Amazon Fulfillment
Poland Sp. z o.o., Wrocław